Hooker Mentality

by Jack Parker

Content Warnings

Sensitive topics are discussed throughout this book which some readers may find distressing. The sale of sex is a major focus by necessity, with some chapters including details about sex acts and associated bodily functions and fluids. Sexual assault including rape is also a recurring topic alongside other forms of violence, ranging from passing mentions to more graphic descriptions from various sources.

There will be segments of this book which tackle these themes from a personal perspective with first-hand accounts from the author. These stories cover selling sex as a teen, interactions with law enforcement, internalized whorephobia, and many other facets of sex work without censoring any emotional reactions to them.

Some of the potentially triggering topics covered in this book are included here, though this list is not exhaustive: rape, whorephobia, transphobia, homophobia, racism, ableism, fatphobia, misogyny, hate crimes, poverty, involuntary psychiatric commitment, imprisonment, etc.

Acknowledgements

This book is dedicated to every hooker I've met who has helped me to form my perspective on sex work and by extension the world. All of you, from the fellow sugar babies I encountered at the beginning to my first brothel mum to the guys who showed me there was a way to keep working after transition, have crafted a community with me that made it impossible to shut my eyes and live in denial. You made me feel at home when I thought I'd end up adrift with no-one who understood.

I would also like to thank my best friend Sidney who has known me for longer than I've been selling sex and who has never flinched away from me for it. You remind me that it is not only other hookers I can go to for support and understanding.

Contents

Introduction

Hookers are incredibly easy to radicalize as leftists. Through this book I do not intend to speak for all sex workers or to say that we all think the same way, but instead to discuss the political issues raised for those selling sex and how we can understand them using a leftist framework. I seek to expose certain commonly-accepted progressive stances as harmful and hypocritical, in addition to challenging the more obvious conservative objections to sex work. An experience of selling sex and an understanding of how sex workers are treated can lead someone to a radically leftist way of thinking purely by observation. Those observations can be written down and preserved for allies who are outside of this sphere, as I seek to do here.

Whilst sex workers may have a wide range of jobs selling sexual services, from making porn to stripping to being a phone sex operator, the focus in this book will be on people who sell sex itself unless otherwise specified. It is vitally important that we promote solidarity between all types of sex workers whilst remembering that the most marginalized have a unique perspective because of our experience of oppression. Other kinds of sex workers are maligned in part by comparison to the most loathsome target who is not considered to be a worker at all: the prostitute, the hooker, the whore. Being a member of this oppressed class leads us to developing a certain mentality to survive. Our work itself also brings things to light, whether we as individual sex workers have the time and resources and disposition to consider them or not.

I was compelled to commit what being a sex worker can reveal about society to paper upon the realisation that even the civilians closest to me do not understand the mentality I have developed through my years as a hooker at all. Almost every thought I have about the state and class and gender and immigration and racism and homophobia is filtered through this lens. This holds true for other sex workers I know, though we don't all come to the same conclusions. If my closest friends who don't sell sex are shocked that I would think sex work reveals so much about all these topics, despite hearing me speak about selling sex and seeing the effects it has had on me in real time, then I have to assume that people who don't have the benefit of a close friendship with someone who is openly a sex worker are even less likely to develop this understanding.

The sex workers I speak to, from all over the world, tend to be radical by necessity. Police treat us in such a way that we often have no option but to distrust them, from which point it is much easier to convince us of the need to abolish them entirely. Misogyny levelled against women who sell sex, and those who do so whilst being perceived as women even if that's not our true identity, is an order of magnitude greater than the bigotry levelled at those who are considered more respectable. Suffering through being treated as vectors of disease who are mentally ill for using our bodies in such a way forces us to think more deeply about pathologization as a tool of control.

When we turn to activism as a way to fight for our rights, we arm ourselves with the words and rhetoric that our allies and opponents will respond to best. What we say in this context is not always the most accurate representation of how we feel. A person does not need to know the currently accepted language or have read entire bookshelves worth of political theory to know when something isn't right. Those who don't want to spend every moment they aren't working on activism have something worthwhile to say, too. Whether they call themselves working girls or a rent boys or hookers as opposed to sex workers doesn't undermine the truth of their remarks, nor does the crassness of their language or the fact it doesn't make for pretty sound bites.

The conversation about prostitution – the term used to legally define our work – is global. Although we are more connected now than ever, I cannot claim to have insight into the ways every kind of culture will impact hookers' views of our work and the language we use about ourselves. My mentality as a hooker is undoubtedly shaped by my own whiteness and Britishness as much as it is shaped by being trans and disabled and working while in poverty. While I seek to cover the nuances in how hookers across the world may feel about different issues, this work has a strong focus on the UK. That being said, sex workers are united by our experiences of whorephobia across borders and identities because of how these attitudes have been exported by colonialism and the ways we learn from each other about how to push back. Differences in culture and demographics and location lead to nuance, not total separation.

As with any group, there are some who bury their heads in the sand and resist the radicalization that calls to other hookers so sweetly. A sex worker who is fortunate enough to love the work and never have a bad client might not consider the systems which persecute their peers. Rich escorts will sometimes pull up the ladder behind them, citing their work ethic and bootstrap mentality as the reason for their success and separating themselves from the rest of us hookers. Others trade sex and experience harm, only to lay the blame on the patriarchy alone and to presume that their feelings on prostitution can be universalized, unwilling or unable to consider that their trauma is valid regardless of whether all sex work leads to the same result.

It's for that reason that I want to talk not about a sex worker mentality, but a hooker mentality. We're all considered hookers the moment we sell sex by people who want to throw the term at us like an insult, but we don't all claim the term for ourselves. Here I use the word as an endearment. I love hookers. They're my people in a way that no-one else comes close to. Under the warm embrace of this slur turned honorific in the mouths of whores, I include those who sell sex without being too ashamed to name it or group themselves in with the most marginalized and reviled. When I speak about hookers, I mean the street sex workers and drug users and unruly activists and those who don't feel the need to use terminology that elevates them above us with the claim that they're a provider of sex who wouldn't dare engage in such disgraceful acts. I am speaking of those of us who may be traumatized and enraged, who know exactly where to direct our anger and do not believe this trauma negates our status as workers.

Someone who has never sold sex can learn from those who have and consider what our industry and the way we're treated demonstrates about society. That does not mean they suddenly embody the hooker mentality that we have built as a mechanism for coping with whorephobia. Understanding where sex workers are placed in the social hierarchy is different from being a hooker who feels it on a personal level. A hooker mentality cannot be turned on and off, added and removed like tinted glasses. It is constant for as long as we continue to sell sex. For most it continues to impact how we think for a long time after, if not until our deaths.

Every time we're denied the right to travel or donate blood or to adopt because of our work, our hooker mentality is reinforced. If we are forced to lie for our safety, the crushing weight of keeping our work a secret only stokes our justified rage. The conclusions I come to throughout this text are rational, but it would be wrong to say that I found myself at this point through utilizing logic alone. It is fury and sorrow and irritation which are ceaseless in the face of whorephobia which do not allow me to look away.

I'm sick of looking to popular leftist and feminist thinkers when I want to make sense of how I'm treated, only to find that if they do not actively detest us then they've never considered sex workers at all. We're relegated to footnotes overflowing with pity and derision from those who are supposed to be our comrades. Any sex workers who manage to gain a small amount of credibility and advocate for ourselves are condemned as too privileged to speak on our work, no matter how much abuse we have actually suffered whilst selling sex, so that people who've never sold sex at all can speak over us on the basis of what they believe they know about the realities of it.

Hooker Mentality

I've heard too many people quote Marx to count, believing they're signalling their solidarity. Scratch one of these Marxists and you find the layer underneath the veneer of camaraderie is one of superiority.

"Prostitution is only a specific expression of the general prostitution of the labourer,"[i] they gleefully quote Marx, claiming his advanced understanding of sex work in an era when it was never considered such, only to leave out the rest of the sentence in his notes, *"and since it is a relationship in which falls not the prostitute alone, but also the one who prostitutes – and the latter's **abomination** is still greater – the capitalist, etc., also comes under this head."*

Marx wrote very little about sex work, thankfully, but what he did write tells us that he found it immoral on the part of the worker as well as the consumer. It is irrelevant that he blamed exploiters and managers more, not least because plenty of sex workers do not have them and did not throughout history, because he reveals his contempt for us regardless. For those willing to delve deeper, his issue with sex workers becomes clear even from the first segment of his sentence. All work is not prostitution of the labourer, in the sense that it does not all involve sex. Marx instead uses prostitution as a synonym for exploitation in a manner that is separate from the way a part of the value a worker generates is taken by their employer, denoting the sale of one's body.

Instead of speaking about selling sex as equivalent to other forms of work, he uses metaphor to share his disgust for the dynamic between capitalists and labourers by comparison to sex work.

In the Communist Manifesto itself, the little writing that mentions prostitution is similarly lacklustre:

"On what foundation is the present family, the bourgeois family, based? On capital, on private gain. In its completely developed form, this family exists only among the bourgeoisie. But this state of things finds its complement in the practical absence of the family among the proletarians, and in public prostitution.

The bourgeois family will vanish as a matter of course when its complement vanishes, and both will vanish with the vanishing of capital."

Marx's fails to see the sale of sex as, first and foremost, a reaction to a need for money in a world where people must earn it to live. The demand is impacted by the way wealthy men feel stifled in their monogamous marriages, their relative power in comparison to women allowing them the time and freedom (and creating the entitlement) to pursue paid sex, however this is always secondary to the willingness to sell sex which is created by financial need. To suggest we must end prostitution and resolve the absence of family among the working class is a fundamental misunderstanding of cause and effect.

Hooker Mentality

Through my lens as a hooker, I am able to see clearly that I would not have lived long enough to agitate bourgeois society and fight back in a meaningful way if not for selling sex. Hookers are paid mostly by men, many of whom uphold the exact systems we seek to dismantle as communists or anarchists, and their frequently ill-gotten gains are transferred to us. We're not all angels who are ethically superior to our clients, though you'd be hard-pressed to argue that hookers are less ethical on average than our clients are. In a way, it's a redistribution of wealth from the capitalists and their lapdogs to the proletariat.

We can infer the opinions of some other left-wing thinkers about full service sex workers through their commentary on pornography and by listening to the arguments they use against it, as with Noam Chomsky during one interview[ii]:

"The fact that people agree to it and are paid is about as convincing as the fact that we should be in favour of sweatshops in China where women are locked into a factory and work 15 hours a day and then the factory burns down and they all die. Yeah, they were paid and they consented but it doesn't make me in favour of it."

"Just like child abuse, you don't want to make it better child abuse, you want to stop child abuse."

Hooker Mentality

It's interesting that someone who supposedly opposes both child abuse and the sale of sexual services so strongly would have interactions with Jeffrey Epstein after he plead guilty to soliciting prostitution from a minor. Then again, when it comes to sexual exploitation and sex work alike, leftists often behave hypocritically.

Chomsky falls into the trap that many leftists do, when discussing sex work; he assumes it is abusive as part of his premise and works from that point, never re-examining his foundational assertion. There are people who sell sexual services like porn who do so whilst enjoying it, for high pay and in good conditions, like fashion designers who adore their jobs and achieve success. There are also those who are coerced into making porn by partners and bosses who expose them to appalling conditions and ignore their discomfort, pressuring them to keep working because they need the money so desperately, like workers in sweatshops.

Hookers notice these differences in ways that Chomsky does not, because we see the difference between ourselves and our peers in better or worse circumstances. Working the street and being harassed by locals and assaulted by clients or police, knowing you have to earn enough not to be beaten by your partner when you return, is not the same experience as working independently indoors with an easy regular client who pays well with a friend in the other room. I know this viscerally because I've felt the jealousy that seeing another worker in better conditions inspires, and I've been so much happier during the brief periods when I've attained those circumstances for myself.

One would hope that well-known feminist writers might have a better perspective, considering the plight of sex workers at least because so many are women who suffer extreme misogynistic abuse and attitudes. Whilst the landscape is improving with more people agreeing that sex work is work and supporting the full decriminalisation of it, there are still many so-called radical feminists who advocate for damaging laws and attitudes.

Among them is Julie Bindel, a writer and radical feminist whose work focuses on male violence against women. In a piece for The Critic[iii], Bindel wrote:

"Accusations of "whorephobia" are increasingly used to silence and deter any criticism of the sex trade. Black, brown and indigenous women and girls are first in line to be bought and sold into prostitution. None of this appears to disturb those apologists on the Left.

On any other issue so bound up with oppression and inequality — a huge, malign free market enterprise that operates for the satisfaction of the exploiter — they would be screaming from the roof tops. You could be forgiven for concluding that the leftist defence of prostitution is indicative of how women at the bottom of the pile matter less than their bourgeois counterparts."

Hooker Mentality

What's most bizarre about Bindel's assessment here is her belief that the left, at large, oppose criticism of sex work and defend it. The people reacting with anger to Bindel's support of the Nordic model (a legal model which criminalizes sex workers' clients and leads to higher rates of abuse against us) are sex workers, not leftists without experience selling sex.

Given her refusal to see any form of selling sex as consensual, exemplified in her book *The Pimping of Prostitution: Abolishing the Sex Work Myth* where she insists it is not a form of work and makes a point to put even the phrases sex worker or sex work into quotation marks, it is not surprising to see Bindel mischaracterise support for decriminalisation and destigmatization as a lack of care for sex workers. What is strange is that she would pretend that there is broad support for decriminalisation, even on the left, when most of the world utilizes some level of criminalisation and that is accepted as the default. Any time I interact with leftists who are not sex workers themselves, I find their knowledge of sex work to be lacking and that they default either to the same client criminalisation that Bindel supports or to suggesting regulation.

Andrea Dworkin was another feminist writer, who Bindel looks up to. She actually did have experience selling sex and spoke about it. Her position on prostitution was that it is intrinsically abusive, and she treated dissenting opinions from sex workers as the product of self-hatred. Her insistence in one speech[iv] that *"the premises of the prostituted woman are my premises"* was surely intended as a show of solidarity with others who have sold sex, but her insistence on exclusively referring to the "prostituted" shows her lack of consideration for sex workers' choices and autonomy, which she considered meaningless under patriarchy.

People quote Dworkin with the insistence that they want what is best for those who sell sex, to protect us by putting an end to the work that many of us select as our best option. As a hooker who isn't fond of selling sex, who has been abused, I rail against this paternalistic mindset. Protecting those of us who do not enjoy selling sex means providing us with the things we're selling it for so that we have no need to. Abolishing prostitution does not feed us, does not clothe us, and does not house us. It simply takes away one more option which many of us prefer to other forms of work that can provide for those same needs. Dworkin's ideas about the intrinsically abusive nature of selling sex are an insult to the intelligence and capability of the women she talks about. When people quote from Dworkin, I think about these later parts of her speech on prostitution:

"The people who defend prostitution and pornography want you to feel a kinky little thrill every time you think of something being stuck in a woman. I want you to feel the delicate tissues in her body that are being misused. I want you to feel what it feels like when it happens over and over and over and over and over

and over and over again: because that is what
prostitution is."

Clients and customers might want to give people a
kinky thrill when they discuss their interactions with sex
workers. Hookers usually don't. We're using our bodies
with intent, not *misusing* them, and agreeing to sex
involving our delicate tissues doesn't suddenly become
damaging when we charge for the privilege.

"In prostitution, no woman stays whole. It is
impossible to use a human body in the way women's
bodies are used in prostitution and to have a whole
human being at the end of it, or in the middle of it, or
close to the beginning of it. It's impossible. And no
woman gets whole again later, after."

This is, in the simplest terms, a misogynistic lie
that mimics the kind of commentary made in classrooms
by conservative teachers spreading abstinence-only
education. I almost expect her to break out their
metaphors, comparing women who sell sex to chewed
up pieces of gum or used tape that has lost its stickiness
and is covered in debris. The hookers I know are some
of the most empathetic people I've met, certainly whole
human beings. I am sympathetic to the idea that
Dworkin speaks from a place of feeling personally
damaged but I find it hard to keep that attitude when
she's applying it outwardly. Anyone who talks about us

14

this way, or who quotes someone who talks about us this way, does not truly view us as equals worthy of consideration. Dworkin doesn't shy away from the topic, yet the things she says about sex workers do us harm just the same as ignoring us does.

There are a great number of people who are victimised whilst selling sex. Some of those people go on to brand themselves as sex trade survivors, rather than rape survivors who used to be sex workers, and label anyone selling sex who does not conform to their victim categorisation as a member of the pimp lobby. It is a difference not simply in what they have lived through, separating happy hookers from abuse survivors, but in viewpoint. What distinguishes sex-selling Nordic model advocates from hooker activists supporting full decriminalisation is our mentality. It's whether we universalise our trauma and refuse to believe someone else might consent to sell sex, or look at the systems governing us and see harm which cannot be resolved by further policing and stigma.

Though I strongly believe that a look at the realities of the lives of sex workers can lead anyone to view our labour as legitimate and to a better understanding of gender relations and consent and racism and the harm done by closed borders, that does not mean it doesn't take work to look at sex work in an unbiased way. Sometimes we need others to guide us and help us seek past the filter our own trauma or disgust might lay over our perception, in a world so full of whorephobia.

I'm proud to be a hooker and I developed that mindset in the arms of other hookers who wouldn't let me slip into an abyss of denial and self-hatred. I found my hooker mentality by listening to people who feel differently about hooking than I do and analysing my feelings whilst fully accepting them. I believe sex workers who love the work, no matter how hard that was to believe at first, and I listen to those who hate it and were abused in ways far worse than I was who don't allow others to tell them that suffering abuse renders their labour illegitimate.

Hookers are sick of being canaries in the coal mine, warning others about rising fascism to no avail. We are tired of being ignored because we are assumed to be too traumatized to know what is good for us. We are done with being denigrated as members of a pimp lobby at the same time we are having the value of our labour stolen by the people we're compared to. Our insights are worthwhile and we are the future of the leftist movement we've helped to build.

Chapter 1:
The Commodification of Intimacy

There is a pervasive idea in many cultures that sex is a uniquely intimate activity. Due to this belief, people view sex as especially horrifying to commodify and therefore equate prostitution to the sale of one's entire body. The ability for many sex workers to experience the sale of sex as a mundane activity, wherever we fit on the spectrum of hating the job to finding it enjoyable, shows us that this view of sex is not objective.

Sex work is not inherently more traumatizing than other kinds of work; sex workers are most often traumatized as a result of stigma, danger manufactured by patriarchal systems, and the predators who are formed as a product of them. To try and argue that the harm is intrinsic, whilst also avoiding rhetoric about our immortal souls that turns off the non-religious, those who look on in horror at our profession point to the intimacy we share with clients as the source of our malaise. They let their hang-ups about sex poison the discourse and call sex work the commodification of intimacy.

Intimacy is commodified in mundane ways throughout the workforce. There are therapists we pay to provide us with support and advice whilst we allow ourselves to be emotionally vulnerable with them and childcare jobs watching over children who come to know their nannies better than their own parents. Compared to divulging secrets during a counselling session or gently lulling a baby to sleep as their temporary caregiver, having a brief sexual connection with a stranger can feel meaningless.

Considering solely this physical closeness and genital contact involved in full service sex work doesn't lead us to a unique aspect to selling sex either. Surgeons and gynaecologists also enter others' bodies for financial compensation. A genital piercer has a far easier time finding the clit than the majority of clients do and frequently spends longer touching it. Midwives become more familiar with their patients' vaginas than they are themselves. Objectors can insist that there must also be passivity and vulnerability to the work, ruling out the comparison doctors and piercers who would be viewed as more akin to dom(me)s than the typical prostitute, to which I reference people who sell their blood, plasma, sperm and eggs for fast cash.

Hooker Mentality

Developing this understanding of selling sex as not being fundamentally different from other forms of labour does not necessitate that we minimize the harm felt by abuse from clients. We need not deny the sense of wrongness that many of us feel from having meaningless sex by essentializing it as a natural reaction shared by all people. Sex workers are not a different class of human with the ability to shut off the feelings about sex that we have been taught to have for our entire lives, though we are more likely to break through that puritanical conditioning over time, and we react to repeated assaults similarly to how any civilian would if they were placed in our shoes.

Other workers also feel the same way to various extents without the baggage around sex, if they work in high stress environments. Add in harassment and you have a recipe for low career satisfaction with high turnover. Junior doctors change professions because the strain of having another person's life in their hands becomes too much. Therapists quit because they find their clients' issues too triggering. Childminders retire early because they can't bear to become so invested in new children who they will never see again once their contract ends. All of these workers are likely to face regular instances of being verbally abused in direct proportion to how closely they interact with clients or patients. I know that it can be difficult for some people to wrap their heads around a sincere comparison between these professions and someone who fucks for a living, but as a person who has always taken on secondary civilian jobs I have no trouble connecting the dots.

Years into selling sex, I began working at a retirement village as a night porter to supplement my income. I earned less from sex work after coming out as trans and found that I struggled more than ever to find enough clients, so the regular income was immensely helpful. As the job began to include more time where I provided disabled residents with care, despite my lack of qualification to do so, I developed connections with them. Sometimes I'd help occupants use the toilet, aiding them in standing and dragging portable toilets into their bedrooms to use. I'd help them to transfer into wheelchairs or stand and use walkers if they were capable, enabling them to make it to the bathroom. I saw residents in various states of undress because they needed support with clothing themselves or with hygiene, all things that were never given to me as part of my job description, and I excelled because I was long past shame or discomfort over nude bodies and their functions.

One resident with dementia often called me through the emergency line in the early hours of the morning, insisting someone had broken in or that he urgently needed to catch a flight to see his daughter. I made him decaffeinated coffee and chatted with him until he calmed down, all while he told me about events from decades ago that he believed were current. Months into knowing him, he walked out into the snow in his pyjamas and I caught sight of him on the CCTV by pure chance. I didn't have to watch it for my entire 10-hour shift, only at intervals throughout the night, but I liked to leave it open on the screen when I wasn't busy with other tasks. I ran out to get him and took him back to his room, but that moment stayed with me. My care for him had been commodified and limited to the times I was explicitly paid to notice his struggles, in the absence of family or friends who could support him for free. I watched the CCTV more closely than ever from then onwards.

There were people in that retirement village who I became closer to than I ever was with my own grandparents. Multiple residents died whilst I worked there and I grieved for one. When people tell me there is nothing more intimate than sex, I think about holding a terminally ill elderly woman's hand whilst she described her pain using the toilet to me. I think about her husband telling me how much he loved her and wanted to give her relief and having to tell him that he could not give her more morphine according to her care plan. I think about holding a man's penis for him so he could urinate into a bottle because he had limited movement and couldn't be moved, his ribs broken after a fall on a night when we couldn't get an ambulance for over 7 hours, whilst he pleaded with me to call 999 for a fourth time to hurry them along. Every single one of these incidents burned these people's faces and personalities into my

21

mind. I'd recognize every single one of them if I went back to that job. I can't reliably recall specific moments with most clients and I definitely wouldn't be able to pick them out of a line-up years after we met.

What all this taught me was that selling sex is not unique to other forms of work in the ways I have been told. I cannot believe that sex is an experience which brings me to knowing another human on the most visceral level possible when I have seen into someone's core much more deeply through their pain as they get close to death instead. There are a multitude of jobs involving almost every single thing that someone could point to and say is unique to sex work. Thus I can come to no other conclusion; the sole way in which sex work is exceptional is that it involves sex and services related to it.

Once we identify sex itself as the point of contention, rather than the potential for close physical and emotional proximity to clients, we can consider whether that is a good enough reason to treat selling sex differently from other kinds of work. Selling sexual services is undoubtedly different from providing haircuts, yet cutting hair is also very different from bartending or underwater welding. To understand sex work exceptionalism, we have to delve further into how consent is treated differently when it comes to sex rather than other activities humans can participate in with our bodies.

Hooker Mentality

A person consents to something when they agree to it. That agreement can be nullified or complicated by a number of things such as age, coercion, and/or mental impairment. There are legal constructs around consent which determine the parameters under which someone can consent to different things. Consent to medical procedures is treated differently to consent to the terms of a workplace contract, and there are separate of laws that cover when a person consents to sex. In addition to the law, the social and cultural frameworks built around sexual consent are highly varied and are not usually created with the sale of sex in mind.

Consent is often viewed as more important with regards to sex compared to other activities. This is exemplified by the common belief that sexual consent must be enthusiastic to count. The same people who strongly insist on enthusiasm during sex seem to have no trouble understanding that a person can agree to a medical procedure or contract that they aren't thrilled about. Since sex workers are frequently unenthusiastic about our sex with clients and yet agree to it because of the financial incentive, we are put in an odd position. Some of us even share these views on sexual consent whilst firmly feeling that we are not being raped by clients we choose to sleep with for money, so we can be left stumped by this enthusiasm requirement without being able to articulate why.

The fatal flaw in the model of consent which requires enthusiasm is that it fails to take contradictory desires into account. Sex workers desire money and so we agree to sex that we otherwise do not want to have – contradictory desires. We also see similar kinds of contradictory desires from people who want to become pregnant but are not in the mood for sex during their ovulation window, who have sex due to their desire for a baby rather than their enthusiasm for sex. Controversially, some people also engage in sex acts with their partners that they aren't personally excited for as a way to make them happy. These sexual encounters might not be the idealized kind of sex people dream of but they do fit under the umbrella of consensual sex.

Separate from the issue of enthusiasm, we have the concern of coercive forces negating consent. A clear cut example would be threatening a person's life if they don't agree to perform a sex act. Under capitalism, when workers must continue to sell labour to survive, there is a less obvious coercive force which acts upon us all. We are pushed to engage in labour that we otherwise would not in an effort to cover our basic living costs. The threat for people living paycheck to paycheck is most significant because quitting a job could result in their homelessness and starvation. Some leftists refer to waged labourers under these conditions as "wage slaves" to highlight this.

All working class people live under this capitalist threat to our lives if we fail to earn money. We can label this as a coercive force. Coercion is one of the factors which negates consent, regardless of whether our model requires enthusiasm. Sex without consent is rape. It is obvious how this logic would lead someone to the good faith conclusion that selling sex will always be a form of rape, for as long as it occurs under these conditions. I could argue back that selling sex alone doesn't feel like rape, without some added factor, but I can see why that wouldn't be convincing when there are plenty of people who were sexually abused as children who would justify their abuse with the same reasoning.

Rather than base my argument on emotion, I urge people to consider the difference between coercion on an interpersonal level and through larger systems such as capitalism. Patriarchy applies coercive forces to women across the globe, who are punished on various levels for not making themselves sexually available to men. Heteronormativity pushes queer people to seek out straight relationships rather than those they otherwise desire. Does this mean that women and queer people are incapable of consent whilst these oppressive systems remain intact? Or do we already recognize rape as a harmful act which occurs between individuals, which these larger systems influence or encourage but do not create by themselves?

To argue that the sale of sex makes something into rape is an argument that sex workers are raped by capitalism. While this might make for a shocking slogan, it is not a useful way to talk about the reality that sex workers face on a daily basis. It also would not make our clients guilty by proxy. Sex workers are highly likely to be raped by clients and police and abusive partners alike using our typical understanding of sexual assault as an interpersonal phenomenon, and conflating these experiences with bookings that we agree to and organize undermines the meaning of rape.

If we frame all sex work as rape, that has some troubling implications. It would mean that sex workers are asking to be raped when we seek out clients. It would mean that when we place our advertisements and sit with our phones desperately hoping a potential client will call or text, that we're looking forward to our own rape. It would mean that when we get a walk-in client at a brothel who we find attractive and who we have enjoyable sex with, that we're happy about being raped and face no psychological repercussions over it.

Of course there are sex workers who see money as a perk for sex they would otherwise be glad to have, and they're fortunate people whom none of this needs to be applied to and who destroy the idea that sex work is inherently non-consensual because of the financial incentive, but those sex workers aren't the majority and it would be disingenuous to focus on them alone. Hookers like me who don't enjoy the work still deserve to have our autonomy respected and to be allowed to define our own experiences. There are many of us who are bored by selling sex or detest it and our consent still matters. Allowing ourselves to be assumed incapable of it does us all a disservice. By considering consent on an interpersonal level and the coercive forces present in society separately, we are able to capture the necessary additional nuance.

As part of not treating selling sex differently from all other forms of work, we must also consider how this understanding of consent fits in with the way we think about other jobs. If we understand that selling sex is not rape despite the existence of capitalism as a system which limits our options with the implicit threat of poverty, we must recognize that viewing other jobs as wage slavery is also incorrect. While applying labels like rape and slavery as metaphors may have some value in causing shock and getting people to think about the role that capitalism plays in their choices, these exaggerations are taken incredibly literally by many radical feminists and/or communists. Confronted with the choice between being owned by another person and selling your physical labour, one scenario stands out as clearly worse than the other. Slaves have no end to the hours they are owned, no alternatives, and cannot exercise their autonomy in basic ways.

Among those who cling to the perspective that waged work is a form of enslavement, customers and clients of workers with an hourly rate like babysitters or decorators are still not scorned as harshly as clients of sex workers. The hyperbole isn't equally applied. Sex workers' clients get labelled as rapists but customers of other workers aren't referred to as torturers or considered complicit in slavery. Softer language is applied because unlike being a client of a sex worker in most places, people aren't discreet about attending restaurants or going to shops where waged employees work. Leftists who use these exaggerations for their rhetoric can't follow through on their slavery metaphor for waged work the way they can for prostitution, because they would be implicated as oppressors by their own uses of various services. None among them can insist they do not participate in the system, however they can easily claim not to pay for sex and get away with it if they're lying.

Although it is important not to falsely refer to all clients as rapists, thereby reducing sex workers' autonomy to being unworthy of consideration, it is also possible to go too far towards excusing the participation of certain clients in taking advantage of the most vulnerable. In some cases, clients are well aware that the sex workers they meet are in desperate need of money and do not want to have sex with them, and they seek them out explicitly because they enjoy that unwillingness. I've known sex workers who've been unable to hold back their sobs while their clients went down on them and I've been practically catatonic as a client kept thrusting on top of me. Our agreement to endure this kind of sex because of financial need does not make me forgive the clients who could have paid us with no strings attached and instead chose to fuck us. Not all sex workers feel the same about our jobs or do them in the same circumstances, so we have to make our considerations individually.

Hooker Mentality

Frustratingly, concerns around the commodification of sex are also sometimes used to frame clients as victims. Lonely straight cis men are the client stereotype, spoken about as an exploited class whose needs for intimacy are used to manipulate them into handing over their incomes. They learn what sex is from porn, are alienated from women, and have no choice but to pay for sex if they want it at all. Anyone who has been selling sex for a significant period of time knows what a lie this is, not least because such a huge chunk of clients are married or have partners. Johns aren't uniquely ugly or repellent in comparison to men who don't pay for sex. Their reasons for paying are typically the ease of finding someone who is their exact type without any preamble to the sex, plus the bonus of guaranteed discretion.

Free sex isn't inaccessible to the men who choose to pay for it. Fundamentally, clients pay for sex because the unpaid sex they can find isn't exclusively on their terms and with the specific people they lust over. Nothing about this makes them victims of manipulation.

One married client will complain at length about his "bitch wife" who dared to turn him down for sex during chemotherapy or pregnancy or whilst grieving a recent death in the family. Another will insist he has been driven to cheat because his boyfriend won't cater to his strongest desires, since he won't agree to be face-fucked until the point of vomiting. Another will complain that everyone he tries to date expects something from him, whether that is the bare minimum of respect or paying for dinner, and convince himself that sex workers are the only people being honest about the transactional nature of sexual relationships. Another will reveal that she has had a bisexual awakening since her divorce and that she wants to explore her attraction to women… with a teenager whom she can relive her youth through.

Most clients aren't seeking intimacy in the only place they can get it by paying for sex – they're avoiding it. Developing mutual sexual relationships necessitates some level of compromise, because no two people are going to have perfectly synced sex drives and equal levels of libido for the precise same kinks and acts. If a sex toy could fulfil all of these desires, plenty of clients would gladly opt for using them instead of seeing the sex workers they objectify regardless.

Not every client has these same motivations, but those who are craving intimacy quickly find that a booking with a sex worker won't give it to them. Like casual sex, though it is instead a professional sort, transactional sex exposes the truth that sex is not automatically romantic and does not produce a genuine emotional connection on its own. For the more intimacy-neutral among the client pool who do not fear compromise with a sexual partner, their motives for purchasing sex tend to be more related to confidentiality and a need for practice. They seek ways to express interests which they might be ridiculed for and model healthy sexual behaviour in anticipation of future unpaid sexual interactions. Bookings with clients like these get us closer to real connection.

It's not impossible for a sex worker to have intimacy with a client. That experience just cannot be sold because it can't be falsified and packaged for consumption. We cannot make ourselves care about a client if it does not occur naturally. A rare instance where a sex worker feels truly close to a client is exactly that – rare. Like an instance of a therapist bonding with someone receiving therapy and feeling kinship with them or a nanny loving a child they care for as their own, the connection between the client and worker exists laterally to the transaction and isn't guaranteed by it. There's no magic formula for clients to trick us into it, either.

Similar desires from two clients can garner wildly different responses depending on the sex workers they see or how those workers are feeling for the hour or two they have together. A man with a recently deceased wife seeking out a woman who looks like her might find a sex worker who views his fantasy as morbid and disturbing as she goes through the motions of getting him off. The next sex worker on the escort directory might find the same scenario very touching, feeling a sense of fondness for her client afterwards when she recalls the affection he had for his spouse that she was briefly a proxy for. The same can be true for clients with taboo kinks who are nervous about sharing them and might happen to stumble upon a sex worker who has the same interest, or they could change their mind last-minute and ask to meet with a different worker who is triggered by the very concept.

Intergenerational divides can be bridged during quiet moments filled with paid sex and conversation just as easily as disgust might be evoked in sex workers who are tired of being fondled and leered at by old men. A client could be difficult to deal with because he is terrified of any kind of sex with another man, since losing everyone he loved to AIDs during the 80s and 90s and absorbing so much fear. Soothing his nerves might feel like a chore or an act of community care depending on the person. I've learned queer history from a handful of clients and counted down the seconds in my head for dozens more of them until they shut up about their pasts.

Empathy cannot be purchased. Workers all over the world express it with their clients, particularly in professions where we are placed into close proximity with one person at a time, and that is a result of humans seeking connection and supporting each other regardless of circumstance. To say that intimacy can be bought is to undermine what it is. What people who oppose the sale of sex are really telling us when they condemn it for commodifying intimacy is that they think it is fundamentally impossible for people not to have strong feelings about sex, instead of understanding the true variation in sex workers' emotions.

Hooker Mentality

Being paid to fake intimacy with clients often makes sex workers expect more from their partners in their personal lives, with the common complaint that we might as well have had sex with a client when we have an unsatisfying hook-up. Faking orgasms to feed a partner's ego feels less reasonable when you're used to having cash placed in your hands to put on that kind of performance. Sometimes civilians try to match this energy but lack the context to make it work for them, instead trying to turn selfish partners into a source of income rather than seeking financial independence and a partner who genuinely satisfies them.

Women are often accused of having a "hooker mentality" when they expect the men they're dating to pay for everything and buy them gifts to make up for a lack of emotional awareness, minimal sexual pleasure, and the rigid gendered expectations within the relationship. This is a misunderstanding of how actual hookers think about personal relationships. I don't want any partner I have to feel like a client. Instead I place value on freedom and mutual loving support. Only in the absence of these things do I seek money and treat our interactions like work. The hooker mentality about relationships means an expectation of actions that demonstrate being a good partner, or else you're relegated to being just another client. We're not mixing business and true romance.

Once again, it is the failure to view our jobs as the work that they are which is responsible for the misunderstanding. Sex work isn't a style of relationship; it's work. By singling it out from other professions, we end up minimizing the ways in which intimacy is a large part of various occupations. Instead of smothering our rage about the injustices sex workers face when we are vulnerable with clients we are in close proximity to, we can consider these issues as part of the larger whole. A system where people must work to earn money to survive does us all a disservice and means that financial incentives taint many of the forms of care we need and leisure we crave. This must be opposed at every level, whether these occupations involve sex or not.

Chapter 2:
Fucking the Enemy

With the exception of a small percentage of sex workers who have the privilege to be selective about the kinds of clients they see, sex workers cannot afford to screen our clients' political beliefs or core values before we have sex with them. Short of sending them a questionnaire which would cause them to balk and seek someone else to hire, there isn't a way for us to *try* to find out, even if we delude ourselves into thinking they would tell the truth. It is a struggle to filter out the serial predators, let alone conservatives.

People who pay for sex frequently feel entitled to it. They are also highly likely to be cis men. Since a significant amount of disposable income is required to become a regular and pay for sex on a consistent weekly or monthly basis, the clients we see are therefore often wealthy and self-absorbed enough to view us as little more than sex objects. Our inability to avoid the most conservative and misogynistic and racist and ableist and

transphobic of these men leaves us fucking our political
enemies.

Once these clients are in our beds (or bending us
over surfaces), it also becomes very difficult to push
back against any bigoted rhetoric they spew during the
course of our time with them. A man who word-vomits
sexist rants about his wife might react with violence to
being challenged by a sex worker who he sees as worth
even less than her. These unequal power dynamics
become more extreme when the sex worker is a member
of a group the client is targeting, but they continue to
exist when a john decides to divulge his bigoted views
about a demographic the sex worker does not belong to.

Being a whore taught me to swallow resentment
like nothing else. I've learned to hide my disgust at
clients' wealth and hateful views, dodging questions
about my true opinions and stroking egos to keep them
sweet. That ability soothes conflict in my life like a
balm and it poisons me every time I use it. Experiencing
this position where you are unable to argue with a client
can leave you feeling choked up and sick. I often war
with myself over whether it's worth saying something to
shut them down, knowing that the majority won't react
with violence or by demanding their money back,
because of the fear that some will. Whenever we call out
bigotry, we take a risk. That risk feels so much higher
when the person I'm confronting is paying me for sex,
which is how I justify staying quiet. I'm not sure if the
risk to me is really high enough that it's a good excuse

for my deflection or silence. This forces me to judge the silence of others just as harshly, who make excuses for refusing to call out their friends and acquaintances despite the lack of this looming threat.

I've lost count of the number of times clients have insisted that it's their wife's duty to fuck them, excusing their infidelity as something impossible for any man in such a situation to avoid. Other clients have told me they really liked my profile and then gone on to complain that too many sex workers they come across are Romanian or Polish. I vividly recall one woman telling me that the only reason she'd agreed to a couple's booking with her husband was so that she could verify he used protection, because people like me are usually diseases. While their words sting like barbs, early on in my time selling sex I kept my expression neutral, swallowing my shame. I stood or laid there paralysed by it. Instances where the bigotry was not directed at me, but at women or immigrants like those I know and love, stuck with me the most. At night I replay those scenarios in my head and imagine how I could have responded.

The money those bigots gave me, which I earned in part because I did not challenge their comments and carefully changed the subject, paid my rent. I'd have been on the streets without it. Every now and again I'd stare at the ceiling, on my soft bed paid for by whoring, and feel the guilt coil around my insides. It has never been sleeping with the enemy that prompts my inner turmoil – it is what they might say to me before and after and during. These days I argue back because my safety has become a lower priority that my sleepless nights.

Xenophobic clients do not spare immigrant sex workers from having to hear these comments, because they pay (less) to see them too and treat them worse when they do. It is my position of privilege as a white British citizen which has ever let me deal with this guilt from a position of relative comfort, choosing to stay silent or offer only weak protests to pay my bills instead of having to stay silent in conditions that are worse so that I don't get reported and deported.

Every sex worker has their own line for what they will tolerate, many doing our best to deter xenophobes and racists and homophobes from contacting us in the first place. It's simpler to place these deterrents than to argue with bigots in the moment, because the effect on our income is not experienced so directly. We cannot know to what extent statements in our profile about meeting clients of any ethnicity or sexuality are resulting in us earning less. These assertions only put off the kinds of white supremacists and homophobes who think a sex worker is tainted by the touch of any man of colour or queer man, so we still end up being contacted by a lot of intolerant assholes who reveal their hateful nature later and are left with no idea what number chose not to book us at all.

Hooker Mentality

Political enemies we do reject tend to be those who are very quickly overt about their prejudices, in part because of what it tells us about their likelihood to act on these feelings in violent or extreme ways. It is extremely rare for a person to manifest a singular type of prejudice to the exclusion of all others, and as a vulnerable group sex workers know that we will be one of their targets. Our solidarity with each other in these moments that clients spout their bigotry can be understood as a path to self-preservation, rather than genuine anti-racism or committed opposition to anti-immigrant bigotry or misogyny or homophobia, the same as when the bigoted opinions shared are directed at us personally.

If a sex worker gets a text from a client where he brings up a desire not to use condoms for oral (common practice in the UK) and follows up this request with saying he is a "clean white gentleman" to incentivize them, we are able to learn two things from the message. First, we learn that the client is racist enough to believe his whiteness makes him more trustworthy and less of an STI risk. Second, we are informed that he is used to using his position of privilege to get his way. Instead of asking the question and accepting the response, he attempts manipulation before he's even done asking. Workers of colour I've spoken to about this phenomenon are extremely likely to tell me they reject these potential clients on the basis of their racism, however other white sex workers will typically lead with the concern that someone who espouses these kinds of beliefs about STIs might stealth them as their reason for refusal – if they notice or mention the racist implications of the message at all.

This cynical view of why sex workers might push back against certain types of bigotry only for their own safety is not a claim that sex workers don't show genuine solidarity to each other at all, merely a refusal of the narratives that some white cis straight workers like to promote. We're not all a big happy family that equally detests the bigots among our client pool. Some of the bigots are within our community. The harm done is not equal and neither are our reactions to it. A white worker can choose to say nothing in response to a client's racist comment to avoid angering him while that same client making the same comment to a Black worker is essentially giving a warning of the potential for physical violence which no response will lessen the chances of. A cis woman selling sex can brush off a client's transphobic comment but a trans person knows an assault could be imminent. Getting to do mental calculations on whether it's worth speaking out is an opportunity that comes from privilege.

Once I came out as trans, I felt this difference acutely. With new articles about trans panic in the newspapers every day, clients would often make jokes about pronouns or say they appreciated me not being as sensitive as those *other transgenders*. They'd misgender me on social dates out in public, tell me that trans people seem to be confused, and speculate on why a trans man might reject his birth assignment. Sometimes I'd be told I had to keep my genitals the way they were whilst a client had his dick inside me.

I'd heard clients make off-handed remarks disparaging trans people before |I came out. Suddenly the comments increased in frequency a dozen times over and turned into disclaimers about the ways they wanted to hurt me and how they assumed no-one else would care. I can't credit my character for leading me to my current understanding of solidarity. I was forced to see it by selling sex as a marginalized person. I understand it because I've lived through being raped and hit by clients who loathe me for what I am, knowing they've made insulting comments about trans people to cis workers before who stayed silent. Blacklists fill up with reports of no-show clients and time-wasters while almost never including stories of clients who spoke about their desires to harm our peers.

As time passes, the way sex workers handle our most awful clients shifts. My biggest change in perspective came with transition, but there are an almost infinite other number of important moments in a sex worker's career. We jump between freeze and fawn and fight responses to clients who evoke a sense of dread within us, no matter whichever we started with. People who used to work with the sole concern of self-preservation become part of a diverse community, finding people we love who we're willing to risk abuse

41

for. Some get pregnant and have children they know they need to get home to. Our self-esteem plummets until we don't care about ourselves anymore. A partner comes into our lives who encourages us not to tolerate mistreatment. Any major life change can become the catalyst.

Many sex workers experience a righteous anger when we hear that other people tolerate so many hateful comments from their friends and families precisely because of our perceived need to tolerate them from clients. We tend to be more outspoken in social settings as a result of being limited elsewhere, whatever our current position on standing up to clients. We have to ask: if we feel so much guilt over not challenging those holding power and money and the possibility of violence over our heads, why is it that so many others feel perfectly fine not calling out their buddies and romantic partners? Their proximity to bigotry is something they have far more control over than we do.

Fucking the enemy, who we know to be bigoted and immoral, does have one major benefit; it's a lot easier to feel guiltless after scamming or robbing them. I've dubbed this practice "Robin Hood hooking" and I've never found a better term. *Steal from the rich, give to the whores.* I don't feel bad pretending my rate is two or three times higher than it really is to a client who I can tell is my class enemy from his expensive watch, nor do I feel the smallest smidgen of guilt when I pretend to use the bathroom and sneak away from a social date where the client's been sharing his far-right stances all night.

Stories of scams and thefts orchestrated by sex workers tend to be shared in the media as examples of our depravity, instead of journalists considering the possibility that we're taking what we're owed from the depraved. We can consider the extra money taken from this type of john to be a tax on them for the harm they do to people like us, particularly when that money goes straight into the sex worker community itself through donations or sharing the spoils with our peers. If only that view were shared by the public.

Working class clients who scrimp and save to be able to afford to see us on a rare occasion, who treat us well or neutrally, aren't worth attempting to steal from. We're more likely to empathise with their money struggles and see them as peers, too. Pragmatically, there's also a risk of reprisal we face when we steal, so we need to rely on our targets being too worried about their reputations to come after us or too rich to care about the theft beyond a wound to their pride. For these reasons, the best clients to steal from are wealthy men who are married and cheating on their partners.

Married men tend to seek out sex workers rather than casual sex partners they do not have to pay so that they can get closer to a guarantee of discretion. Both the sex worker and the client are incentivized not to let the affair become public knowledge. If the client is careful enough, he can make sure the sex worker has no

identifying information about him at all, so there's no
chance of his partner being contacted. One too many
stories about mistresses finding their boyfriend's wife
on Facebook can make them paranoid. In the face of
that, why risk everything over a lost £50 deposit or
leaving his hotel with his wallet emptied of cash?

The actual ethical question many sex workers
reckon with over their clients being married is not
related to whether they can morally justify stealing from
them. Instead, it relates to being a participant in their
infidelity. Sleeping with someone isn't going to turn
them into a bigot, nor will it worsen the bigotry that
someone already holds, but sleeping with someone *is*
the deciding factor in whether or not they've been
unfaithful.

Since so many people start selling sex out of
sudden necessity, there are many of us who don't think
about the ethics of sleeping with married or partnered
clients in advance. Some sex workers are hit with a
sinking feeling when they see a wedding ring on a
client's hand as they're about to be fingered, as it occurs
to them for the first time. Others flash back to painful
memories of being cheated on when a client mentions
having a boyfriend at home who will wonder where he
is if he stays any longer, left in the dark about his
proclivities. We're all trained from a young age to have
scorn for mistresses and secret gay lovers and home-
wreckers, who we sometimes see more anger towards

than the partners who do the cheating, and it can be hard not to apply that disgust to ourselves.

It's impossible to maintain this initial horror about involvement in infidelity for long, particularly in the face of client's shamelessness about it. These cheaters aren't being unfaithful because we tempted them somehow; once they've decided to seek out a sex worker, they're going to find another if we turn them down on the basis of their relationship status (which most won't bring up). We have no culpability for having consensual sex with a person who made commitments we were never part of, entirely separate from us. There is no sense of duty to be observed towards our client's partner unless they are someone we know and would otherwise have to lie to about the cheating.

I've participated in discussions with many people who've been hurt by their partners engaging in infidelity, who are nominally sex worker allies, where inconsistencies in their opinions are revealed. They argue that being the third party to cheating is wrong but make an exception when I bring up selling sex. Their excuses start and end with the reminder that selling sex is my job rather than a recreational activity. To that I say: that's terrible reasoning. Plenty of professionals do immoral things with the excuse that it's their job, like cops and engineers creating tech that is used to kill people. If something is wrong then it doesn't become less so when you're paid for it. Relying on sex work for my income forces me to confront the ethical question at its core. I also can't make the excuse that I don't have other options to make money because that isn't always true. I could alleviate myself of guilt in times of struggle, using a similar argument to liberals who won't condemn theft only when the person stealing is trying to avoid starvation or feed and clothe their child, but it wouldn't hold for the times I'm less desperate. If I concede that what I am doing is wrong, yet claim should be exempt from judgement due to circumstance, there will always be a line where I become morally culpable. Perhaps that line would be when I've already covered my rent and bills for the month and I'm riding married men's dicks to afford a gaming console? That line has been crossed in my working life more than once.

Agreements of exclusivity are the business of those who make them. It does society no good for me to turn down sex with someone on the suspicion that they're cheating. Frankly, in some cases I'm sure I've spared exhausted partners from being pestered for sex again by the insufferable man I'm dealing with instead. Whatever their personal situation, if I don't know it then I can't make judgements on it. What would be the benefit to protecting a relationship I am not privy to from a partner's attempt at disrespect, if they are already set on breaking their promises? The moment the client tries to make a booking, surely they have already committed an act of betrayal regardless of whether I turn them down. It is not the act of the sex itself which makes them guilty. This placement of blame firmly onto the cheater can be applied to any kind of sex between two people where only one has a monogamous partner. Whether we're talking about casual sex that occurs purely because of attraction and horniness or sex workers making our living, the lack of fault is exactly the same.

I didn't expect slinging pussy and hawking mediocre blowjobs for cash to lead me to solidarity with the lovers of married and partnered people. I ended up there by being honest with myself about the logical conclusions to my arguments. With this commitment to my position, where my hooker mentality leads me, I find myself having arguments with my peers who also sell sex almost as often as I argue with civilians. I do so because it is more honest. We cannot afford to be hypocrites. If something is wrong on a fundamental level, payment doesn't render it suddenly acceptable. I won't permit the irrational excuses people make because they know selling sex wouldn't pay enough without married clients in the same way I'd dismiss anyone who told me they had to work for an arms manufacturer to pay their rent. I would not work a job that is immoral.

Separate from adultery, there are some scenarios in which fucking the enemy is ethically stickier. Are there situations where letting someone pay us for sex might actually encourage their harmful behaviours? When I was 18 and working as a cis woman, did my clients feel emboldened in their misogynistic entitlement towards women as a group after I let them throw me around like a rag doll and bruise my cervix whilst holding back my complaints? It's an idea that radical feminists like to throw at us, but it's also a question I've organically had that I think a lot of sex workers struggle with.

A portion of clients see sex workers as being akin to very advanced sex toys. They dehumanize us in their minds, treating us like blow up dolls or fleshlights, and get a sense of satisfaction from our objectification. The word no is irritating to these clients, and more often than not they brush it off and cross boundaries into sexual assault if we begin to deny them or refuse certain acts. This kind of abusive client often targets women and thinks of them as being inferior, though there are also those who have sex with men who are effeminate and visibly queer and hate them for that flamboyancy. Violence is enacted against sex workers by these clients in a way many of them would argue was incidental if they could be pushed to admit to the harm at all, because they don't think of us as people whose feelings matter. When this inconsiderateness doesn't cross the line into assault, it is due largely to luck that the sex worker isn't opposed to the acts the client is interested in or the roughness he exhibits.

Sex with a man like this comes with a special brand of shame that's unique to being a hooker – the sinking feeling that we might have validated this behaviour by making ourselves available to him for sex and that we've *profited* from making him worse. It is deeply unfair to suggest that those of us who are being objectified and mistreated should be blamed for the harm abusers go on to do to others, however unfairness is not the enemy of truth. The real antidote to this shame comes with experience selling sex and seeing countless numbers of these men who we learn with time are not so easily swayed. Sex workers are shown over and over that abusive and misogynistic and homophobic men, who are already set in their ways, target sex workers precisely because they've already settled into their predatory behaviour and are choosing the easiest targets.

Men are not taught that it's acceptable to harm women when they pay them for sex; they already believe it. They believe that these sex working women, who they degender through objectification and mentally hyperfeminize in equal measure, are a female sub-class who they can get away with abusing and unleash their abusive fantasies upon. Each time a post on social media goes viral suggesting that incels should be sent to see sex workers or claiming that incidences of rape drop when paying for sex is accessible, it is an implicit admission that people understand this. The men who mistreat and assault women they've paid for sex were going to abuse women regardless, and seek out those involved in prostitution because they can get away with it since the police and general public do not care.

With every new happily married family man who is outed to the sex worker community as a serial rapist, we learn this lesson again. Predatory men are not created by people who tolerate certain levels of mistreatment for cash, stumbling into becoming rapists. They are controlled. They save their desires to sexually abuse others and exert self-control until they unleash them on people who are considered disposable. Formative experiences that have occurred long before they call us to their hotels or show up at our incalls are what have made them this way. Validation from their peers is the icing on top of the shit cake. Agreement from their buddies means far more to them than a transaction with a person they don't even view as human does.

Refusing entitled clients is another way sex workers prove to ourselves that sleeping with these men isn't the root of the problem. They react with rage and insults to polite rejection. "You think you're too good for me, you stuck-up bitch?", "I'll rape your cunt for that attitude", "What do you mean, no? You're a whore, it's your job." They have a confirmation bias that makes them view everything women do through a misogynistic lens and everything queer men do through a homophobic one. Our acceptance or refusal to have sex with them is irrelevant because their perception will warp to fit their hateful world-view.

As for whether paying for sex might turn a man who is not mired in sexist thinking into an overt misogynist, the idea is absurd. Paying a woman for sex doesn't make a man believe he is entitled to sex from women. He's likely been taught from birth that he's owed sex by virtue of being a man. Money is a condition sex workers are placing on sex, just as a condom or a refusal of specific acts might be from someone who doesn't sell sex. A man who pays a woman for sex and respects that condition isn't engaging in an act that would lead him to respect women as a whole any less; he is following at least one boundary.

On average, men who pay for sex lie somewhere in between committed intersectional feminists and unashamed predators. They're painfully average. What sex worker hasn't been chatting to a man in a social setting and thought some variation of "this guy has client vibes" due to his demeanour? This idea that sex-buyers find themselves on a pipeline to depravity from the moment they text a number they find on an escort directory ignores the reality most sex workers face. Our clients are usually boring and indistinguishable from the other men we know to a startling degree. We can imagine our fathers and bosses and friends and co-workers and acquaintances as clients because after long enough in the industry we've had at least one client who acts like them. This is true to such an extent that it often invades the way we feel about befriending and dating (mostly cis) men in general. Seeing the same in people of other genders is rarer, experienced mostly by those providing niche services to a less typical client base.

On dates with trans people or cis women that go poorly, I believe I feel the same kind of disappointment as my friends who have never sold sex do after a bad date. I lament how unfunny I was and the awkwardness of the silences, obsessing over whether I should have gone for a kiss at the end of the night or if it's for the best that I didn't. On dates with cis men that go poorly, my instinct is to be frustrated that I went out with them for free. The strength of this frustration intensifies more if I had mediocre sex with them. If I skipped the date and sought out a hook-up over Grindr during which I went into work-mode and failed to prioritize my own pleasure, it becomes rage.

Over take-away at the brothel I've heard other workers tell me that they don't have casual sex with men at all anymore, because it's so often indistinguishable from the kind they have with clients. Sitting on the grass at the local park after the Sex/Work Strike in London my friend told me that she didn't want to come out as a sex worker to her brothers, just in case she'd be able to tell from the looks on their faces that one or more of them had paid for sex before. At the same time, she said she was scared they'd stumble across her profile by accident if she didn't. Chatting to people at a social event for sex workers, I ended up talking to one acquaintance who told me that he'd only been dating women because his experience in sex work had been deeply traumatic and he couldn't help but think about all men the way he did about his clients, despite being bisexual with a preference for men. I don't match these behaviours myself, however I do understand them.

Early on in my time selling sex, I found myself most baffled by sex workers who often had clients they *liked*. Like many of my peers who began selling sex in difficult circumstances and with little idea as to how to do so safely, I believed that the way my clients acted was universally applicable. I failed to consider that the kind of men who would fuck a teenager less than a third of their age would be especially abusive. Not only do sex workers have to reckon with fucking our political enemies – sometimes we also struggle to realize that not all of our clients meet that description.

I've noticed the same phenomenon from a lot of sex workers. It's not that we hate all our clients, but that even the ones we feel mostly neutral about are still paying us for sex when we'd prefer to have the money without providing the service. When you've been sexually assaulted a number of times, as many sex workers have, the idea of sex with an unenthusiastic partner can feel triggering or uncomfortable even when it's entirely consensual. Hookers struggle to place ourselves in our clients shoes, and the idea that they might delude themselves into believing we really enjoy being with them can be unsettling.

The client who caused me to re-examine my dislike towards all johns was himself a former sex worker. He was attractive and exactly my type, a decade older than me instead of several, and I saw him for the first time when my top surgery had been scheduled but had not yet occurred. This attractive man chatted to me about his cat and décor and put me at ease. He didn't ask me to take off my binder or make a single uncomfortable comment about my body. Finding him so charming was incredibly disarming to the point that I forgot to pinch the tip of the condom and found myself profusely embarrassed when he had to remind me. My muscle memory from having had hundreds of clients before totally failed me. We had sex that I found genuinely enjoyable to the point that I willed myself to take a mental snapshot of his head between my legs to get off to later. I told him what a good time I had, which he laughed about and rebuffed with the reply that I probably say that to everyone, and I realized it was the first time I'd been completely genuine.

    Later I found this former sex worker turned client on Grindr by chance and struck up a conversation. We hit it off and I started to hook up with him for free. Only once we'd met again casually did he share his past experience selling sex at my age. I cannot stress enough how out of the norm this was for me. Pre-transition I felt sick at the idea of spending a moment longer with clients than I needed to and I was exhausted by performing for them. I almost never liked the sex, with rare exceptions that I still found off-putting in some way. I truly believed this was the experience all sex workers had until I transitioned and realized that my overwhelming discomfort was at least partially related

54

to my transness. I hated the sex and I hated my clients however kind and considerate they were because they were viewing me as a woman. I also projected past trauma from my years hooking as a homeless teen surrounded by predators onto men who were doing nothing wrong by being attracted to me.

Breakthrough over, I began to view johns differently and stopped assuming my peers were in denial when they said they had a good time with a client. Through listening to them, it became clear to me that sex workers can enjoy sex with clients, but that most of us don't because we aren't becoming hookers out of a love for sex with strangers. There's a selection bias happening, not something inherent to the sale or purchase of sex itself. Most of those who start selling sex do so because we are lacking in other options, not because we've always dreamed of it, so the chances we happen to end up enjoying it by co-incidence are slim.

Knowing how likely it is that any sex worker a client books will feel this way about selling sex, we are still left with a sense of wrongness. There is no perfectly ethical way to consume products or procure services in a capitalist society but there are still more and less ethical choices. People who pay for sex are treating their erotic pleasure as more important than the potential distress a sex worker might experience. Beyond the question of consent, which sexual partners are capable of providing even when unenthusiastic, we have the question of fairness. Clients have the funds to spare for

this kind of leisure activity whilst sex workers are in a
position of needing that money and having to tolerate
discomfort to provide it. They could offer this money in
lieu of requesting any service at all, and I personally
think they should, yet they'd never be in proximity to
the sex workers they pay if not seeking them out for sex
in the first place.

A person who pays for sex is suspicious to me
because of their priorities. However, in the world we
currently live in, full-service sex workers rely on a
constant influx of clients to get by. Each time the
demand drops, so do our earnings and therefore our
ability to survive. Clients aren't heroes for parting with
their money, their goal being to cum rather than to keep
us fed and housed, but it's difficult to see them as worse
than the people who make other kinds of work
inaccessible and push us into selling sex even when we
don't want to. Bosses who won't hire us and people
with money to spare who won't part with it are not
superior because they keep their distance and don't see
the effects of their choices.

Men aren't all the enemy and nor are all clients.
The capitalistic white supremacist cis hetero patriarchy
is the enemy, as are its foot soldiers who can be found
among clients and people who've never once paid for
sex, and those who are complicit. What we should be
focusing on, instead of exaggerating the importance of
sex, is how we render our enemies ineffectual and take
their system down. Earning enough to house and feed

ourselves by fucking them for money in the meantime is how many marginalized people survive to be a part of that fight.

None of us are automatically radical for who we fuck and nothing has shown me that more clearly than selling sex to men I'd never give the time of day in other circumstances. What can make us radical is the context we fuck those people in and what we do after. If someone's politics rubbed off on you by shagging, sex workers' clients would be far less shit than they are. We aren't tainted by fucking the enemy.

Chapter 3:
Radical Honesty and
Tactical Lies

Regardless of how entitled and sadistic many people who pay for sex can be, the average client doesn't want an unenthusiastic sex partner. For the majority of sex workers who do not love the sex we're having for work, this leads us to the common business practice of faking enjoyment and pleasure with our clients to keep them happy. Lying is a tool that we can use to protect ourselves from sex buyers who would respond with violence to our honest thoughts, as well as a way to entice them to return. We lie about our real names to build a buffer against stalking. We claim false ages and misrepresent where we live or what else we might do for work or schooling. The one thing we can reliably be open about with clients is that we're sex workers.

Our need to lie does not end with clients. We're further pressured to keep secrets when it comes to our loved ones and those with power over us. Families and friends might disown us due to the shame associated with prostitution. Anyone in a position of authority could destroy our lives by making our jobs public knowledge. The core self is fractured between the work persona we use with clients and the more natural personality seen by our social circles. Both groups lack awareness of fundamental parts of our lives. Neither version of ourselves is allowed to be fully authentic.

Because of the incentives to hide selling sex and our feelings about it from almost everyone else, sex workers are prone to saving total honesty for each other. There are a thousand ways a hooker can justify lying to a pimp or a client or family members, but those excuses don't apply to people in the same situation. Risks that still exist when sharing information about our work with peers are entirely overshadowed by our burning need to tell someone about such a stigmatized part of our lives and to support each other. Secret meetings with other hookers might be the only place we can share our truest selves, unmasked and unashamed. Once we share that we sell sex, so many of our other private thoughts come tumbling out after.

Taking a look at how sex workers determine who it is safe to be radically honest with, as well as the calculated risks we take to be open with others even when it's dangerous, can serve as a lesson for progressives who are secretive out of simple fear of judgement. Though sex workers are put in a position where sincerity with each other is rendered necessary, we can note how it would be beneficial regardless of the these compulsions. Every social boundary crossed about what is acceptable to disclose brings us closer.

Taboos become much easier for sex workers to break with each other, even when we are strangers, because our lives are taboo already. We give out the gory details of experiences that non sex workers might never be open about. Forbidden subjects become fewer and fewer. This is particularly true when the relevant taboos are a result of systems which oppress sex workers, thus giving us no reason to respect them because we don't benefit. To pick an obvious example, sex workers have a propensity for ignoring the social rules enforced by patriarchy.

If a sex worker tells a story about using a make-up sponge to stem the flow of blood on their period to hide it from a client, other sex workers are far more likely to share their own hijinks hiding their menstruation than to wrinkle their noses in disdain. No gasps of indignation about the impropriety of the conversation permeate the room. I have heard sex workers go into graphic detail about their mishaps using all sorts of products from baby wipes to flexible menstrual cups, offering vivid descriptions of the sensations they felt during sex with them in, with no more hesitation in person than in groupchats where they can remain faceless. These same conversations may happen within progressive groups of civilians, relegated to bathrooms or DMs between close-knit friend groups, but they regularly fail to take place out in the open. Hookers skip the requirement for a level of closeness to get into the bloody and explicit particulars.

Discussing STIs is another topic which becomes less embarrassing when surrounded by people who have had a much higher number of sex partners than average. No prevention methods against sexually transmitting an illness are 100% effective besides complete abstinence, which full service sex workers are obviously not practising, so we have to develop an attitude of acceptance to the possibility of catching an STI if we spend a long time in the profession. Admitting to offering bareback sex will still get negative reactions in plenty of sex worker spaces depending on the norms in a given location and among the demographics present, but catching an STI is far less likely to have you treated as a pariah when others around you are also in a similar boat.

If you are not a sex worker and you catch chlamydia or syphilis or any of the host of transmittable illnesses which are primarily communicated through sex, your best source of information on the topic is likely to be your local clinic. Friends might provide you with emotional support if you tell them, although equally they might view you as dirty or disgusting and spread the information as gossip. Unless you're fortunate enough to have friends who work in sexual health, who are otherwise educated about the topic as a result of their queerness, or who are from a group that is heavily impacted by stigma around these illnesses, the risk of being open about such a diagnosis is often not worth it. You might be considered tainted by future dating prospects or have the information spread among these so-called friends. Sex workers have additional motivations to be honest about our sexual health without the same drawbacks.

By sharing symptoms which could be STI-related with other sex workers, we gain access to the collective knowledge of the community. Some sexual health clinics treat sex workers awfully, so asking other workers is often the only way to avoid discrimination. We can seek advice on which clinics will allow us to get more regular testing done, since many of them don't allow testing more often than every few months but make exceptions for people who are at a high risk. Through personal experience, other sex workers become sources for advice about how/whether to inform past clients about their potential exposure or what additional treatments can soothe discomfort.

Abortion is yet another issue that sex workers are forced to confront, with the possibility of an unwanted pregnancy as a common looming concern for many of us. Unlike people in serious relationships or who have casual flings on occasion, we deal with the potential that a pregnancy could result from a booking with a client.

That adds a lot of extra concerns. Any fertile sex worker with a uterus who is one condom split away from an accidental impregnation knows the fear intimately. We have to approach it with humour or by being casual about it to cope. Sex workers have always covertly organised abortions with the help of our peers and the first step to getting one is telling each other.

The first time you hear a hooker joke about blackmailing a client to get some extra cash in return for terminating a pregnancy, it might catch you off-guard. By the tenth time it becomes too routine to garner more than a light chuckle. The shame gets absorbed so much that people will talk about what they would do if a client got them pregnant, unprompted, so that they can use other sex workers as a sounding board. I feel the exact same way about anecdotes involving drug use to get through bookings that are equal parts funny and tragic.

Candid discussions about drug use among sex workers are unfortunately more limited in where they take place than conversations on other topics. They're hushed, including when we're able to retain our anonymity on social media or through published works, because of negative associations between selling sex and using mind-altering substances. Every time I talk about doing lines of coke with co-workers at a brothel so we could more easily stay awake and peppy for late night clients, there is a pit of worry in my stomach over what stigma it might contribute to. This applies tenfold for users of the most demonized of drugs like heroin.

Hooker Mentality

Among those of us pushed into keeping our drug use private, we see impediments to where we can go for advice. Particularly for our more niche problems, we only have each other.

If you want someone to console you because you were too high to feel the friction-induced soreness from too much anal with multiple clients, another sex worker who uses drugs is your best bet. Almost no-one can be all but guaranteed not to judge you for using drugs to help dissociate through transactional sex besides someone doing the exact same thing. Add in the usual dynamics that exist between drug users like keeping in contact to share information about dealers or to share drugs when one person hasn't been paid yet and you have a recipe for close connection. That's without factoring in how some drugs lower our inhibitions and make us more honest with the people we seek out while high.

Overlapping taboos will leave us with the most stark difference between what we are radically honest about with each other and what we hide from public view. An example of this would be a situation where someone contracts an illness commonly seen as an STI through needle sharing whilst using drugs. Many civilians will take this sort of information to their grave with them. Conversely, sex workers frequently experience a compulsion to divulge.

As HIV is the most stigmatized of the illnesses labelled as sexually transmitted infections and which is associated with drug use, sex workers who are HIV+ may only disclose their status to others in their exact situation. Once someone with HIV is in treatment and their viral load becomes undetectable they cannot pass it on. Despite this, other sex workers who should know better often react with horror at the idea of a HIV+ sex worker continuing to have sex with clients. Campaigns to inform people that U=U (undetectable = untransmittable) have been spreading the word about the reality, but the attitudes that were cultivated during the 80s and 90s still hold strong in society.

For sex workers in treatment for HIV, hiding their status from clients is one of the few options available to them to make ends meet financially. The average client is far less knowledgable about STIs than the average sex worker is, so with an awareness of the ignorance within the community itself it should be obvious that they tend to react poorly. Knowing they are not putting anyone else at risk of contracting HIV, a tactical lie or omission to a client can be the difference between being able to put food on the table or not. How robust the sexual education is in a given subset of the community and whether we're talking about sex worker activist circles or peers working in the same area will change a lot about who HIV+ workers are open with. The streets are a very different place to a leftist hub.

As we've established, subsets of sex workers are likely to share more with those who belong to the same demographics as them when they're at risk of stigmatization from within the community. Racism from white sex workers towards sex workers of colour and clients alike is prevalent in plenty of places, especially in countries with majority white populations, so sex workers of colour have been known to form their own activist groups and events for this reason. Inter-community racism turns this into a necessity so that they can express themselves.

There are countless profiles for sex workers based in the USA with the stipulation "no AA" (meaning no African Americans) in their lists of client expectations, and less coded requests of "no Black men" from sex workers in other countries too. The people using these phrases typically try to justify their racism by saying they had a bad experience. Curiously enough, these same sex workers never seem to ban all white men from seeing them when they have a bad experience with a white client. Calling out these widespread racist practices can be stressful for sex workers of colour and leave them fearful that they will lose access to resources and community if they say something. Being honest only with those in the same position at first can be a vital way to gain support.

Sex workers of colour in countries which do not have majority white populations are still silenced on the global stage, if not from inside their own communities. Their openness about the struggles they face are ignored, punished because of racist attitudes, or held up as supposed proof of stereotypes. This can lead to a heavily curated public presentation of the sex worker rights struggle in their activist spheres. They differentiate themselves from the radical roots of the other sex worker organising that is taking place in an effort to claim the respectability that gets them listened to. As you would expect, this leaves the most marginalized feeling unheard.

Venues such as brothels often have implicit rules about only allowing one or two sex workers of a specific ethnicity to work there at a time, with racist third-party owners treating sex workers of colour like novelty acts. Through deliberate isolation, these workers are deprived of the ability to be completely open with colleagues in similar situations. Employment protections are non-existent when the work is criminalized, including anti-discrimination laws which protect individuals from harassment and inequality in the workplace over characteristics such as race, and public discussions about discrimination from sex work venues seem to only place the focus on clients.

Another subset of sex workers who are more honest within our community than outside it are trans sex workers. Cis women in the community are especially likely to speak as if all of their peers are also cis women, largely because they make up the majority and find it easier to generalize, which leaves us ostracized when our experiences don't quite fit. Detailing too many of our exploits to cis sex workers can scandalize them and cause them to question our

genders. Once we factor in that there are certain crimes
we are likely to engage in that other sex workers are not,
to access HRT or as a result of archaic laws regarding
gender segregated spaces, we have a recipe for some
fracturing and a need for trans-specific spaces.

DIY hormone treatment is common among the
entire trans population and sex workers are no
exception. The major difference for us is that we are
even less likely to be able to access medical transition
legally. On top of the gatekeeping by doctors that
restricts the average trans person from accessing
treatment through the legal routes, our sexual history is
used to claim our dysphoria must not be severe or that
changing our sexual characteristics is not in our best
interests. The additional barriers faced by trans sex
workers mean that we are almost all doing some level of
personal alchemy without state approval.

How could we not share tips on combatting
vaginal atrophy from testosterone whilst being
penetrated by multiple clients in a day, or varying doses
of estrogen and using Viagra with clients who insist on
being topped? Our doctors won't help us because they
often view our sex work as evidence that we aren't
really trans in the first place, so we have to help each
other. In some of the most frustrating cases, therapists
and GPs may even insist that selling sex has traumatized
us to the point of making transition seem more
appealing. If any element of our transition is impacted
by sex work, we have to work out an alternative excuse

for the issue we are bringing to our doctors so that they'll be willing to treat it.

Both misogyny and fetishization from clients can have psychological impacts, but the idea that they can induce someone to become trans is bizarre and stems from arguments popularized in the 18th and 19th century about sadism from clients causing lesbianism and gender non-conformity among sex workers[v]. Clinicians who buy into the idea that engaging in sex work should exclude someone from transition-related care are signalling their belief that it can be an external cause of gender dysphoria. They not only believe transness may be caused by trauma, but that it is more likely for a cis person to be made trans by engaging in sex work and becoming traumatized than for a trans person to end up in sex work of any kind because of societal factors. When gender therapists have already made up their minds that choosing to sell sex is evidential of damage to self-concept and identity or an inevitable cause of it, trans hookers are obligated to lie to them for our own well-being.

Doctors supposedly know best about our health, yet sex workers are consistently worse off when we tell them the truth. Admitting that we lie to them is yet another way sex workers value supporting each other with the truth over what might be viewed poorly by others, in turn exposing doctors' biases for what they are. We are taught not to trust someone just because they went to university and earned a position of authority. This mindset is adopted not only by trans sex workers keeping our professions secret from gender therapists, but by all sex workers keeping our jobs a secret from a variety of people with power.

Renting is a minefield when you can't admit what your job is to your landlord. Bank statements can be used to prove the amount of money being earned on a regular basis, but for most full service sex workers who are being paid by clients in cash that means our deception as renters has to begin months before we start the referencing process. We have to pay our earnings into the bank without getting flagged, inputting reasonable increments and having a plan for what we'll say if someone calls to question where our cash deposits are coming from. Once we build up evidence of our income, we then need a fake job to tell our landlord that will pass muster.

What jobs can we pretend to have without making it look suspicious that we're only paid in cash? Will this job sound stable enough that our landlord won't reject us out of concern our income might suddenly disappear? Endless work goes into crafting backstories and explanations for where our money is coming from because the truth would be damning. Some sex workers looking to rent opt to create fake contracts and use friends with company e-mail addresses to falsify their way into a home without showing bank statements, breaking the law to skip the hassle. People don't want to rent to prostitutes. The rare few who would otherwise consider it end up being put off by the legal ramifications they'd face if caught. The need to lie forces us to confront the ridiculousness of the rental system in its entirety and builds on our resentment towards landlords.

All this lying has to happen so that we can live in a home that is likely filled with issues our landlord is too cheap to fix, which we pay for by selling sex. We put money in their pockets by being fucked. Our alternative is telling the truth and ending up homeless, under which circumstances selling sex only becomes more dangerous. Beyond the equal objections any worker may have to landlords profiting from housing scarcity and the inherent unfairness of paying off someone else's mortgage while gaining no percentage ownership over the home, hookers have the additional issue of being undesirables whose cash is seen as tainted. The housing market seeks to dictate more than how much we must earn; it dictates *how* we earn it. The ease with which we can lie to the same people who want to determine the way we live our lives further exposes their incompetence.

Bosses are no harder to mislead than landlords. Sex workers fill in our CV gaps with stories about caring for sick family members or make up work histories to claim we have the same experience and skills that we really developed through seeing clients. According to most people we're supposed to pull ourselves out of prostitution and get real jobs, except those same people don't want to hire recently retired sex workers or take a chance on applicants without an employment history, so a few falsehoods are a necessity to meet their expectations. If these necessary lies are revealed during our employment, our bosses' beliefs in the stereotypes that sex workers are manipulative and a poor choice to hire are reinforced. It's rare that we're allowed to keep our jobs if our past comes to light.

If we succeed in falsifying the information we need to so that we can stay housed and obtain at least a part-time income outside of selling sex, we still have a multitude of other systems to navigate. Religious leaders must be kept in the dark so that we can continue to worship with our local community if we are religious. Social services must be avoided at all costs and have sex work hidden from them, lest we be considered unfit parents. We're worn down *before* we start keeping secrets from those we care about most.

Having such a constant need to lie to people in our lives about our work provides context for why so many of us seem to word vomit information that anyone else would guard as a secret. When we're not chatting about pregnancy scares, abortions, drugs, and STIs, sex workers are often going into excruciating detail about our bodily functions and those of our clients and partners. We go beyond what many people share with friends and family because sex workers often lose the ability to distinguish. The hooker mentality can be very

all-or-nothing. If you're a fellow sex worker, you get all
the gossip.

Ejaculate getting into the eyes is an event worthy
of gathering the group to tell the story, only for other
sex workers to chime in with their gruesome accounts of
clients whose cum was streaked with blood or smelled
strongly of chemicals. I have three different stories
about brown cum seared into my mind forever.
Awkwardness about discussing bowel movements melts
away in the face of so many of us needing advice on
how to perform a quick enema or otherwise prepare for
a booking involving anal. Every group of sex workers
includes at least one who has topped a client with their
dick or a strap-on and suffered explosive diarrhoea
across their bed sheets or those of the hotel they're
staying in. We often justify telling these stories by
saying we're doing it for the good of our friends and
peers. Surely it's worth any discomfort from being open
about it to make sure that other sex workers buy
themselves a waterproof mattress protector?
Nevertheless, if I am totally honest with myself, I find
that I share my own stories more for my own benefit
than for anyone else's. Keeping it all in makes me feel
like I'm about to explode.

Not everyone experiences these strong desires to
share the truth of what they go through and I have no ill
will towards people who are very private, but I would
be remiss not to acknowledge the less justifiable
exception to the general trend towards radical honesty

among sex workers. It comes from those who harbour significant shame over the sexual nature of our work and from high earners with classist views. Their deceit is not always conscious because it often includes lying to oneself as well as lying to others, yet the effects are the same. They keep quiet about their income and the nature of the work they do because on internalized whorephobia.

Labels like escort, courtesan and provider all exist to obscure the sale of sex. In scenarios where we have to contend with criminalization when we advertise, we can't outright admit to selling sex and thus cannot use the words which call attention to it. This begs the question: why do some sex workers continue to use these terms in situations where that obfuscation is unneeded? Criminalized sex workers will avoid these words because they fear reprisal form the law; what do others fear, such that they cannot even name our profession?

Wealthier sex workers are likely to use some of these euphemisms to denote their class, whether intentionally or subconsciously. Although the words someone prefers cannot be used to deduce the rate they charge with perfect accuracy, those calling themselves working girls or rent boys can generally be assumed to earn less than someone claiming the title of courtesan or provider. This language can also give us an inkling as to how comfortable a hooker is with their profession. If they're in denial about being a sex worker at all, as some sugar babies and escorts are, you'll never hear them self-describe with the more offensive labels.

Throwing around accusations of internalized whorephobia at affluent sex workers could be misconstrued as the product of jealousy, so I will use myself as an example of someone who was inclined to use language in this way (despite earning relatively low sums). When I first began selling sex, I maintained a state of denial about what I was doing. I told myself that I was a sugar baby selling my time and that the sex I had with my clients was incidental. Never mind that it wasn't sex I wanted or enjoyed, which I only had for financial gain – I told myself that in theory they could have kept paying me even without the sex, because the expectation was implicit rather than stated outright. I wrapped myself in the cloak of being a sugar baby and sneered at the idea of being viewed as a prostitute. The lies I told myself spilled out of my mouth and I misrepresented my work to everyone I knew.

For our communities to propagate the radical honesty we are internally known for, we each have to work through our classism as well as our associations between sex and shame.

Within many sex worker social circles, the prevailing wisdom is that not sharing rates allows us to avoid confrontation between workers who charge less and those who charge more. If no-one speaks about their rates, we avoid the possibility that one sex worker will make a bigoted comment to another. I've heard the mantra a hundred times, "no rates in the space", and each time I wonder who it really benefits to stifle discussion about our pay.

Classism and whorephobia collide to create the idea that selling sex is a degrading act which can be mitigated or made empowering if only sex workers charge enough. Those who have rates on the low end of the spectrum and have close physical contact with clients are placed at the bottom of the whorearchy in the eyes of non sex workers and sex workers alike. Despite this, low-earning sex workers tend to be very willing to share our rates because of the ease with which others can look them up if we use online ads and work independently. If we do not work in this way, we are still strongly incentivized to share because of our desire to assess how typical our prices are. It is usually the wealthier amongst us who push for an avoidance of sharing rates, purely because they find it uncomfortable to acknowledge the disparity.

Prostitution is not the only type of labour where workers are discouraged from sharing our income, but it's always disappointing to see people who should be breaking these taboos upholding them in place of employers. It's also interesting to see how the aversion to talking about money holds stronger than almost anything else. In sex worker spaces which proclaim themselves to be proudly anti-capitalist and yet will not permit me to say that I've lowered the cost of an hour of my time to £100, I can hear one of my peers laughing about getting throat gonorrhoea for a second time while another details the texture of her shit during a scat fetish booking. I learn viscerally that capitalist conditioning to keep workers from contextualising our income and developing class consciousness is stronger than almost anything else.

Whether it's my friend wondering how long he can keep seeing clients before his pregnancy becomes obvious or another sex worker detailing what to eat and drink to develop maximum gas for a client who's into farting, sex workers' tendency towards radical honesty can teach us something just as much as where the line gets drawn. I can't say exactly where that line is, but it's usually somewhere before me admitting to earning £15 per quickie at the brothel (depending on the crowd).

Left-wing activists can be very guarded and concerned with operational security, for good reason. Worries about spy cops are based on real dangers. What needs to change is not the level of awareness of these hazards, but how they are weighed up against the benefits of freely sharing information with allies. Sometimes an admission to breaking a law is the only way to convince a new person that it's relatively safe for them to do so too.

The things related to our communities that make leftist activists the most uncomfortable to discuss will not all be the same as those that sex workers need to talk about. Instead we benefit from radical honesty about the limitations to our activism, our shortcomings in living up to our ideals, and the amount of work we really do to progress our causes. Environmentalists should talk about the difficulties that come with with avoiding plastic or the times they give in and order something from Amazon. Anarchists should admit to the difficulties they have reaching consensus about contentious topics and the times they've taken the solution into their own hands. All kinds of protestors should commiserate over their aches and pains after a die-in or a march that exhausts them instead of bragging over their tiredness like it's a badge of honour.

It's also important to be extremely honest about one's politics when organizing because it's the only way to find those who share a similar mentality. When left-wing people won't share ideas that are considered extreme, the broader movement stagnates and becomes populated with people who only want to see minor changes from the status quo. That means: being upfront about not just wanting to see illicit drug use fully decriminalized, but not seeing it as inherently bad in the first place; insisting that police are not simply a last resort but are no option at all; being loud about sex work as a form of work which should be included in discussions about labour rights and class; advancing youth liberation regardless of fear-mongering and the infantilization of teens; speaking up when someone else in the movement is being transmisogynistic.

Like sex workers differentiate ourselves from our oppressors, those with these kinds of views should learn to open up fully with comrades and hide their political leanings entirely in situations where it would only do harm to be honest. Leftists can lie tactically to employers and landlords in much the same way that sex workers lie about our professions, wearing clothes that don't give away their affiliations and leaving work for progressive organisations off of their CVs. Where to draw the line is complicated only by the question of when we have a moral obligation to try to spread our ideals even if we take personal risks by doing so.

Family members and friends are more easily reached by us than by strangers, especially when it comes to emotional appeals. Conservative loved ones might react negatively to leftist talking points, however the discussion occurring at all creates the possibility that their minds will change. At the same time, financial dependency on parents or partners or friends is a damn good reason to hesitate in rocking the boat. Expressing a view on a controversial topic is dangerous in direct proportion to how intimately connected you are with it. The larger and less specific complaints, like broad condemnations of capitalism and concerns about climate change, also put leftists at far less risk when speaking than a person of any political alignment admitting that they personally engage in a stigmatized activity. That relative safety persists even when a leftist is directly advocating for the rights of a population like sex workers, compared to if a sex worker admits to being one. With more distance comes less stigma.

Hooker Mentality

Keeping these nuances in mind, it can be hard to judge whether we're keeping our mouths shut for good reasons. I know how easy it can be to convince myself I'm justified when it benefits me to believe that I am. One of the ways we can explore the blurry delineation between when it is and isn't reasonable to lie to those close to us is by considering the situations in which sex workers keep the truth from our most intimate partners. In an effort to protect ourselves from bigotry, many sex workers guard the secret of our profession from those we date or marry.

If you'd asked me my opinion on this kind of lie when I was 19 and first began working in brothels, I would have categorically condemned any sex worker who kept their job a secret. Back then, I still held onto some unrealistically romantic notions about the nature of relationships. My internalized whorephobia was too strong for me to empathize with hookers making the best of complicated situations I had never been in. I also felt too broken to date. Since then, my fellow sex workers have shown me the nuance by being honest with me about their difficult choices and the reasons they made them.

There was a woman at the first brothel I ever worked at who was more than twice my age. She had four children who were all still dependent on her and her husband, all of whom she'd immigrated with to the UK only a few years before. At the start of every shift, she'd show up wearing a uniform fleece with a logo on the upper left of the chest and a backpack containing a packed lunch. Naively, I initially assumed she was coming to the brothel directly from an overnight shift at a warehouse job. I didn't think to ask about it until she complained to me one morning that she'd been in too much of a rush to eat breakfast. She described herself waking up late and complained that her husband hadn't woken her, therefore revealing that she couldn't have possibly come from a late night shift. Once I questioned her over my conclusion, I remember she laughed before she told me that her uniform wasn't real. It was designed to fool her husband into believing she was traditionally employed so he wouldn't know she sold sex instead. She was surprised I hadn't assumed that from the start.

This woman had become my brothel mum. If a client unsettled me or treated me poorly, she was the person I went to for comfort. She reminded me to take my medication. She taught me little bits of Polish and I explained what clients meant when she got texts that she couldn't decipher. On days when I forgot to eat or did too much coke to have an appetite, she'd pull me aside and tell me I wasn't seeing another john until I'd eaten one of the pastries she'd lovingly made for me and the other workers. The idea that she would do something which struck me immediately as immoral was hard for me to accept. It was the culture of radical honesty we'd developed in the brothel that made me confident enough to ask for an explanation, knowing she'd tell me the truth.

What she told me was that she started selling sex at 14 to provide for herself and her sister. She met her husband a few years later and told him everything, to which he promised that he would provide for her financially so that she'd never need to sell sex again. That worked for a short while. Eventually he began to struggle to earn enough to support them and their living expenses went up with every child they had. Moving to the UK was supposed to help him to have access to better job opportunities and pay, except the higher cost of living ended up causing more difficulties and they struggled more than ever. She didn't want to compromise on her children's education or their extracurriculars, which were the first thing on the chopping block for cost-cutting measures as far as her husband was concerned. Ultimately, she told him she'd found a full-time gig at a warehouse. After many years as a stay-at-home mother, my brothel mum went back to selling sex.

Why she chose to lie rather than be honest with him was obvious to me before she got to that part in her story. He was too proud to admit he could no longer provide. Their marriage had long shifted from the kind of passionate relationship with frequent and spontaneous sex, so she avoided it for weeks and months at a time and slept with him during breaks from the brothel after STI tests that came back clear. The rest of the time she talked him into using condoms under the pretence that birth control didn't agree with her. I wondered how much of him remaining in the dark was due to intentional denial on his part rather than her skill at deception. She was coming home with cash that was inconsistent in amount and far too much for the work she was supposedly doing. How could he be that oblivious? I couldn't find it in myself to care about the answer back then and I still can't. My brothel mum was doing what she needed to do to survive, to give her children the kind of childhood that she never got to have, and her husband was content in his ignorance. The lie worked to everyone's benefit.

Not every sex worker who lies to their partner is in a situation quite like hers. There are those who start doing sex work in secret so they can earn enough to leave their abusive partner, with the knowledge that confessing could result in deadly violence. Others get tired of being treated worse by everyone they try to date than before they became a sex worker, feeling like they're always on a countdown to the moment their latest lover decides they aren't willing to share anymore. Some reasons are better than others, yet that exact variance is what demonstrates that lying to a romantic and/or sexual partner is not always equally wrong.

Sex workers lying to our clients is an expectation they share, making it exempt from the same scrutiny applied to romantic partners. Regular attendees of strip clubs are mocked by their friends if they believe their favourite stripper genuinely likes them. We ridicule clients who seek to live out their Pretty Woman fantasies with their favourite escorts, given that they're literally paying for a performance of enjoyment. To blame sex workers for our deception is essentially a complaint that we are too good at our jobs. In cases where the issue goes past faking pleasure into lying about aspects of our personal history, we must also consider the power dynamic created between client and hooker and the perspective that clients aren't owed the truth. Honesty costs a lot more than they pay for an hour of our time.

Laws and guidance which treat people as rapists for keeping secrets from their sexual partners are inevitably used to criminalize sex workers, who (as we've discussed) only lie to protect themselves in the first place. This is especially true when it comes to sexual offences around "deception as to sex"[vi] and how they impact trans and intersex sex workers. Policies like these place an unreasonable burden on trans and intersex people to inform our sexual partners of our medical history, meanwhile no such burden is placed on cis perisex people who are allowed to rely on assumption. As people who have far higher numbers of sexual partners than the average, whose medical histories are not the business of clients merely paying us for services, we are placed in situations with these unreasonable expectations often. We are then condemned equally in situations where we lie or omit.

Hooker Mentality

A trans or intersex person who does not sell sex may be confronted with the question of whether they feel an ethical compulsion to disclose their medical history or anatomy to a partner beyond what is readily apparent, but sex workers have to face this question constantly and are often not in a position to opt out. We cannot rely on celibacy or only sleeping with people who are guaranteed to be accepting. The question of ethics cannot remain unanswered for us.

Here is the answer: consent from sex partners is not undermined by secrecy about any information which is not directly relevant to the sex acts performed. This does not make every omission or lie *acceptable* or work as a dismissal of the ways a person can be harmed by lies from someone they are sleeping with, but it does form a foundation that does not label all stealth trans people as sexual predators. We must instead consider these scenarios on a case by case basis.

Whatever genitals a person had at birth is not relevant to sex that involves the genitals they have now, if they've been altered. Complaining that you weren't informed about this surgery is no different to complaining that you didn't know the person who just gave you a blowjob had their tonsils removed years ago. Someone telling you to close your eyes and putting something different inside you than you agreed to, whether that's a toy or genitals, *is* a violation of boundaries directly related to the act. We can apply these standards to all kinds of lies a person might tell, like a 40 year old saying they're 35 or a red-head not admitting their hair is dyed. It's okay to be upset if you have a preference for natural red-heads or people close to your age and you feel that your sexual partner misrepresented themselves – it's just not the same thing as a sexual assault.

When civilians lie to talk someone into sex, there's also an understandable creep factor. Falsehoods about wealth and status to appear more desirable leave a sour taste in the mouth. Sometimes these lies go on for so long that they absolutely cross the line to become a form of psychological abuse, as with the UK police officers who used false identities to sleep with left-wing activists and even fathered children with them[vii]. Particularly in relationships, abusers will pile on lies and keep secrets with the active intent of manipulation. The same motivations do not apply to sex workers. Both within and outside of sexual relationships, we must delve into the basis for why people lie.

In the end, the ability to safely be honest with everyone to an equal extent is an immense privilege born of conformity. These same privileges protect them from consequences when they do choose to lie. A person who is part of the majority and naturally inclined towards the norm can speak freely without fear of reprisal and punch down when they like. It is the oppressed and those who are condemned for our lack of adherence to model citizen archetype who are hated. We are the ones for whom honesty really is a radical act and who must lie tactically to ensure our longevity. We don't owe honesty to our oppressors and we benefit from providing it to each other.

Chapter 4:
Navigating Civ Jobs

Non sex workers are often called "civilians", so their jobs outside of sex work also end up being called civ jobs. When active sex workers become employed in these jobs either part-time or as a sole source of income so they can stop selling sex, there can be a bit of a culture shock. The difference in hourly earnings between selling sex and doing another job that doesn't require specific qualifications can be stark, as can the lack of flexible hours and sudden bureaucracy. Once you factor in the delay between working and getting paid and the difficulty getting hired in the first place, it's no wonder that even people who don't enjoy sex work will end up going back to it rather than holding down a traditional job.

Fundamental shifts in how we view all work occur for many sex workers, because of our participation in the underground economy. There's rarely a way to undo it.

Hooker Mentality

As someone who is used to exclusively selling sex, entering the civ work force means learning all of the social and legal rules associated from scratch. Applying to a brothel might involve a quick introduction and a few selfies or having a fellow sex worker vouch for you, meanwhile securing an interview for a basic minimum wage job can require hours of work constructing a CV. A friend's word no longer serves as a satisfactory reference and without a work history which can be shared with the new employer, it can be hard to be considered no matter how simple the work is.

Taboos around sex work lead many people to believe that selling sex must be worse than their civ job, to the degree that they won't even consider it. It's a non-option to them. When sex work is someone's normal, it's much easier to compare the mistreatment in other work environments to what occurs in brothels or strip clubs or from clients when working independently. If we're supposed to accept that sex workers are so uniquely mistreated, a belief that those in the industry also absorb, we're going to balk when we encounter worse treatment in a civ job! We might be put off before we consider making the switch just from the stories our friends tell us, struck by the thought, "I'm a *hooker* and I don't get treated that badly."

During one attempt to quit selling sex for good, I got a full-time job as a bartender. The first thing I noticed was that the managers there treated me worse than the brothel owners I'd worked for and that they exerted far more control over my time and behaviour. I've worked in brothels where they expected a very fast turnaround between clients or where I was required to see a certain total number in a day to keep my spot, yet no-one forbid me toilet breaks or insisted I be visibly busy every second I was there. The mantra "if you've got time to lean, you've got time to clean" felt demented. My co-workers accepted it as a standard part of retail work.

Not every civ job is alike, with some allowing more freedom than others, but a constant theme is that work you don't need qualifications to do gets you treated the worst. There are self-employment opportunities outside of selling sex which allow similar flexibility to it, however the downside is that those tend not to be lucrative until a lot of time and effort is expended or money is invested upfront. Guess how most sex workers build up savings for those upfront costs, so that they can switch careers? By doing more sex work until they've managed to earn enough.

Civ jobs are lauded by so many as evidence of stability, so the other thing which drives so many sex workers out of them is the realization that it's still difficult or impossible to make ends meet with the earnings from a full-time civ job. That is, if we can even get one that offers guaranteed earnings rather than a zero hours contract nightmare. The stigma that comes with selling sex doesn't scale 1:1 with how much of it we do, so occasionally selling sex to supplement a civ income leaves us soaking up all the same bigotry on top of the added stress. Unless we have a reason to need a civ job besides the pay, like as a reference to rent somewhere, having to do at least some sex work makes it far too tempting to fall back into it as a main source of income. Unlike people who've never broken the taboo and crossed the line into the sex industry, we're a lot less likely to be willing to go hungry so we can avoid resorting to illegal or stigmatized forms of work. For me, returning to full-time sex work can be the result of something as simple as needing a new TV.

These difficulties with working traditional jobs also lead to resentment of rescue programs intended to help those who want to leave sex work to do so. While the barriers to accessing these jobs in the first place are a real problem and can be mitigated by anti-prostitution employment programs, such as explaining our CV gaps and the lack of skills we can justify or advertise ourselves as having, we're unlikely to stay in the jobs found for us when they pay worse and still involve constant mistreatment. A brothel worker who previously worked 5 shifts a month isn't likely to be able to perfectly adjust to a 9-5 schedule and a 40 hour work week with a snap of the fingers. That applies doubly if we're disabled or have children we're arranging our working hours around. We're likely to quit from exhaustion or end up fired.

Hooker Mentality

You can't really get fired from being a hooker. Brothels can stop scheduling you for shifts, clients can stop calling to book you, escorting directories can ban you, but there's always a way you can keep selling sex. It is always accessible, depending on the level of danger a sex worker is willing to accept. Throwing up an advertisement on a new site can gain you an entire new clientele who don't remember whatever reputation you built for yourself before. Finding a new brothel can be a fresh start because it's not as though most of them are asking for previous work references.

Fucking for money is not easy. Its accessibility comes from the fact it doesn't require extensive training or education to begin. When capitalists are talking about this kind of work, they call it unskilled labour. They call it this because there is no need to invest upfront in training up new workers to replace the previous ones if they're fired, not because the workers do not develop specialized skills during their employment. Almost anyone can take our place at a moment's notice in a brothel or on the street to be managed by a third party.

The skills that are developed over someone's time selling sex can be for the worker's benefit or mimic those acquired by any person who spends time working in sales. Learning about the law and how to stay safe, developing an accurate model for threat assessment, honing the ability to dissociate during uncomfortable experiences; these are all skills that are purely self-serving. Marketing skills like putting up advertisements and charming clients into becoming regulars are useful for independent sex workers who work indoors, however these proficiencies see little use by sex workers who are controlled by third parties or who work on the street where clients find it much harder to suspend their disbelief that the sex worker they're meeting with loves the work.

Sexual skills, on the other hand, frequently have precious little impact on the equation. Pay may be offered inversely to skill or experience, with high-end hookers seeing less clients than those struggling to make ends meet and new sex workers being sought out to a higher degree because of the fetishization of their potential naivete or innocence. Besides sex workers who charge premium rates for physically demanding pornstar experiences, the ones making the most are selling their inexperience and being sought after for their low client volume. Many clients want a sex worker who will allow themselves to be acted upon rather than an active participant. They may intend to give specific instructions which anyone who can moan on command and has a modicum of flexibility and mobility can follow. Skill only increases what a sex worker can charge when the client wants a specific kind of experience, such as being dominated or a face-fuck with a sex worker who can control their gag reflex. Mine are more often titillated by the fact I choke.

The accessibility of selling sex is one of the major reasons that disabled people flock to it. Not only can we work inconsistently without being barred from returning when we're able, but we can work in ways that suit the needs our disabilities leave us with. When I require a cane to walk and deal with severe pain, I meet clients at an incall or take a taxi directly to their hotel or home so that I barely need to be on my feet. Chronic insomnia can't stop me either – I choose my own hours.

Self-employment includes far more jobs than only sex work, however the combination of the demand for sex and the risk and stigma associated with providing it can make it one of the better paid jobs under the umbrella. It is also ethical in ways that benefiting from the labour of others as an intermediary, as recommended methods for earning passive income do, are not.

For some of us, selling sex can be described as a job that is practically tailored to our requirements. It is immensely accommodating for people with ADHD, as one example. The potential danger we could face from any new client keeps us more focused. Last-minute bookings induce a sense of urgency. Our inability to form habits the way neurotypical people do can cause us to struggle with maintaining hygiene standards, so the fact it's much harder to forget to shower or brush your teeth when someone's going to shove their tongue into your mouth and your asshole later is a bonus.

Though it might seem counter-intuitive that autistic people would also prefer sex work to other options, because it involves interacting with people so closely and a lot of touch that those with sensory issues could struggle with, there are actually far less social norms that need to be observed with clients than in most workplaces. If an autistic sex worker chooses to seek clients independently rather than through a venue, they can develop scripts for interacting with clients and not have to worry about how they're viewed by a boss or co-workers. Furthermore, social pressures are absorbed differently by many autistic people, so they tend to be more capable of eschewing the shame pushed upon sex workers. This leads them to be more likely to consider selling sex as an option for reasons other than necessity, if sex is something they enjoy and can imagine themselves providing on a paid basis.

The impact of neurodivergence on the choice to sell sex cannot be overstated, but physical disability is just as much of a major force for leading people to it. Physical disabilities push people out of other kinds work work, limiting us both in terms of the physical labour we are capable of and which employers have unpacked their ableism enough to hire us. I don't want to downplay the sexual skills that many people have learned to get themselves repeat clients, yet I have to note that there are plenty of johns who just want someone to lay there and be acted upon and make some encouraging noises of pleasure. That's something people can do in situations where their mobility and energy are extremely limited.

In countries which offer payments to those whose disabilities keep them from working, there are often extensive rules about how much the disabled person can earn or have in savings which make selling sex an attractive option. Since books are usually paid for in cash, this money can be used to purchase assistive devices which are not covered by the healthcare system without being denied the benefits payments they need to survive on a daily basis.

When the subject of degrading work is raised, prostitution is often top of the list. If you're a disabled person who has both sold sex and begged for government support, you might order that list differently. Through hooking, it becomes easier to see that dehumanization during sex is not fundamentally worse than dehumanization at the hands of the state apparatus which sees disabled people as a burden on all of society. Being subject to constant disability assessments and expectations to live on the poverty line forever because of an inability to join the traditional workforce is exhausting. To say that selling sex feels less degrading than that is not a positive claim about sex work – it is a condemnation of the way our existing systems treat disabled people.

Depending on the disability, sex work can be one of the few jobs besides motivational speaking and disability advocacy where someone's disability might actually be viewed as a positive. This leaves many disabled sex workers having conflicting feelings because of the ways they were pressured into this line of work, making us resentful despite our potential enjoyment of it.

There's a fine line between appreciation and fetishization, which clients cross more often than not. That doesn't need to obscure the positive moments in their entirety. Amputees and people with limb differences can find clients who want to spend most of their bookings rubbing lotion on their stumps. Wheelchair users might have clients who are excited at the prospect of watching them transfer out of their chair and onto a bed, and act which can be a source of shame in the presence of other sexual partners. Upon delving into the psychology of these johns we might find that their reasons for enjoyment are related to arousal at signs of struggle or helplessness, however this is not always the case and we cannot read their minds to know. The seasoned hooker knows not to let themselves absorb what clients think of them into their self-concept, and instead to make the most of the good moments when they come.

The fetishism of disability that does occur whilst selling sex tends to be blatant, because clients are paying for the privilege to break social norms, although it is already very widely accepted to harass disabled people in a number of ways. A change in the style of the ableist comments or actions does not necessarily correlate with an increase in the severity. Outside of sex work, workplaces are frequently full of co-workers who will ask inappropriate questions out of curiosity mixed with bigotry. Those can be more frustrating because of the lack of openness. It can be more difficult to process ableist comments from someone who claims to mean well than it is from someone who you know is making those comments because they're aroused.

Any job that is accessible in the way that sex work is, in addition to having a disproportionately high number of disabled people involved, will also have higher numbers of undocumented people doing the work. Without a work visa, immigrants who do not have the legal right to work in the country they've come to are limited to cash in hand work or employers willing to take the risk. Of these possibilities, sex work is one of the most lucrative.

While documented immigrants with the right to work may seem like a group who would have an easier time navigating traditional jobs, racist and xenophobic employment discrimination still leaves them weighing up their options. Workplaces are likely to be filled with citizens born in the country they're working in and it can be difficult to find companionship or to stand up to mistreatment for being an immigrant in these environments. People from a particular country or region might flock to a profession to concentrate themselves there and build a community at work to mitigate this, like with care jobs. Venue-based sex work is known for this too.

Among all of these groups, it is women who sell sex to a disproportionate extent. The overlap between

misogyny and other forms of bigotry practically
guarantees it. Women have always used selling sex as a
means to earn an income when denied equal access or
equal pay in other fields of work. We see artefacts of
this past and present reality everywhere despite the lack
of effort made to preserve sex worker history or capture
women's voices, often in the form of texts which
condemned women for using one of the few ways
available to them to earn money without a father or
husband to provide.

Before the creation of the internet or telephones,
women were able to signal their willingness to sell sex
with clothing choices when they went out in public and
by writing requests to brothel madams who would
employ them without any skills or level of education.
Those who were illiterate could ask friends for aid, turn
up at the brothels in person, and in some cases go to the
police to register as prostitutes and ask for placement in
a suitable brothel. Servant positions often required a
level of propriety these women were considered unable
to uphold because of their reputations. A major factor in
this was whether they had children out of wedlock.

Since then, in places where women have gained
more legal rights, one of the major factors making sex
work more accessible to women than other jobs
continues to be its viability for single mothers. The
flexible working hours mean these women can sell sex
whilst their children are at school instead of having to
pay for a babysitter or after-school program to

accommodate the longer working hours typical for a civ job. Summer holidays and half-term breaks make up more days than almost anyone can take as vacation from traditional employment. Conveniently, sex work can be done sporadically. Children can be left with a partner or a friend at night to solicit on the street without the young one ever noting their absence, as opposed to missing milestone moments because of a day job. Women embarking on parenthood isn't punished by the underground economy in the same way it is by the rest of society.

Efforts towards legalisation, in place of the full decriminalisation of sex work, are fundamentally attempts at rendering sex work less accessible. Legal models come with regulation and punishment of those who will not or cannot comply. Who has time to get a license for selling sex when they're made suddenly homeless, if they'd be granted it at all? Why should people be forced into selling sex at a venue rather than their own home, when that leaves the physically disabled at the mercy of brothel owners to make the buildings accessible? For what reason should additional time and effort be spent by people who are highly likely to be engaging in a profession out of necessity?

Client criminalisation has a similar impact, reducing our client pool and therefore making sex work less viable as a primary income source. Crucially this doesn't stop us from selling sex, instead making us desperate and increasing our willingness to see the most dangerous clients to make up the difference. We start trading away our boundaries in service of avoiding civilian jobs that would be worse or because they won't hire us anyway. Sex workers who don't feel comfortable offering anal see that as the only way to upsell to the few clients they have left. Others meet with johns who've abused them before, knowing there's no-one new to supplement the lost income that results from banning them. The clients who keep reaching out to make bookings become too nervous of sting operations to give out their personal information, making them nearly impossible to screen.

Whatever complaints I have about sex work (and I have many), it is clear to me that the people who choose to sell sex would be worse off if it was not accessible. I cannot view civ jobs as a better alternative in all cases. In the absence of access to funds through other means, or when a civ job would not meet my needs, I become viscerally aware that I prefer to be fucked by someone I am not attracted to than to starve. I am primed to understand that the accessibility of my work is incredibly important *and* that it only pays enough for me to make a living whilst remaining so convenient because it is stigmatized.

I cannot be angry that selling sex is available to me as an option. What I am is full of anger over how difficult it is to afford to exist as someone who struggles with civ jobs. I am furious that something I do not enjoy and am judged for is all I'm left with. It has taught me never to settle for less than total accessibility in everything, because of how sex work so acutely highlights this injustice. I hope that others will demand the same.

Chapter 5:
Surveillance and Research

State surveillance is ever-increasing and a person who sells sex has good reason to avoid being monitored. Sex workers are canaries in the coal mine when it comes to every form of new technology built to find people and record their interactions. Facial recognition is used to deny us the ability to cross borders, police observe us on street corners and by raiding brothels they've known about for years when they finally decide they want to terrorize us, and our communication over social media can be accessed under the guise of fighting against trafficking.

As the use of AI for facial recognition becomes more commonplace and the technology is developed further, sex workers are one of the groups it is weaponized against first. For advertising purposes, those of us who work independently have to include pictures of ourselves on escorting directory websites that are popular and therefore easy to find if we want to secure a high number of clients. Countries like the US have a policy of disallowing entry to anyone who has sold sex in the last decade, so they can easily justify keeping a database of faces found through these escorting advertisements which they use facial recognition software on. We're a convenient group to test this new technology on with a massive pool of faces to choose from.

Border patrol employees are not the only ones with access to facial recognition programs. The average person can match a sex worker's persona to their real self, if there are face pictures attached to both identities online, by uploading a single photo to a website built for the purpose. Since the introduction of pictures to the internet, the possibility of a sex worker being recognized has existed. Facial recognition multiplies that risk a hundred times over.

I can use this software to search my own face and scroll and see links to my personal social media right next to directories of leaked nudes which include those I posted on OnlyFans or Reddit years ago. I've deleted my old accounts, yet the pictures and videos were downloaded long before – mere days or weeks after they were originally posted. My estranged parents, who denounce me for my job to the rest of my family that I no longer speak to, can track down any new escorting advert or porn profile that I make. Online crushes of mine who I flirt with can go and find videos of me masturbating to decide if they think we'd be sexually compatible based on the act I put on for viewers, instead of talking to me about my interests and desires.

As violating as it is when someone I know uses this technology behind my back to view sexual content of me without my permission, it is the impact facial recognition can have on sex workers' future job prospects and safety that worries me the most. Significant numbers of us work in caring professions whilst selling sex on the side. Our bosses finding out about our sex work would be career-ending. Immigrant sex workers I know risk deportation if their sex work is revealed through someone finding their ad. Stalkers, who sex workers collect like we're a magnet for them, can use a picture on our work account to find any other images of us on the internet and learn our real names or other places of work.

Before any excuses about catching violent people through CCTV footage can reach the ears of sex workers who advertise online, we are taught to fear facial recognition technology for how it can be used to harm us. That guides us towards siding with other potential victims of it, as well as making us more invested in allowing all people to maintain their privacy.

Limitations on travel imposed as a result of facial recognition are one way that sex workers who are not immigrants are given a rare insight into the appalling mess that is border control, uniting us in our opposition to state surveillance of non-citizens. Border control officers frequently stop sex workers when we are attempting to enter other countries as tourists, having discovered that we are sex workers through intelligence gathering processes which are intentionally left a mystery to us[viii]. The US is particularly known for this, due to their policy of disallowing any foreigner to enter the country if they have sold sex in the last decade.

Methods used to avoid detection include being "face-in", including no pictures of our faces in escorting advertisements, however sex workers may still find themselves in databases of known sex workers after taking these precautions because of the requirement to show our faces and IDs to verify our ages on the most popular sites. Pressure from the police and government officials causes some sites to hand over sex workers' personal information, meaning that our passports may potentially be shared with foreign governments so that we can be blacklisted.

Whether or not becoming known to our governments and others as sex workers can be avoided by those who advertise online, we can minimize the chances that anyone else is able to link our work to our true identity by never sharing identifying pictures or information on personal social media. As recently as a decade ago, sex workers were giving each other the advice not to post the exact same selfies to personal and work accounts to avoid anyone tracking us through reverse image searches. Now that advice has morphed into the instruction that we must not post pictures of our faces anywhere else if our face is shown in our ads, alongside the suggestion that our personal accounts should be private and restricted to only our friends. We have lost the right to a personal life that we can share publicly.

Using completely separate devices for our professional and personal lives is also widespread among sex workers as another way to avoid being caught. Very few things will make you as aware of how hard it is to be anonymous online as trying to set up accounts as a sex worker will. Nearly every app will try to connect to the contacts in your phone or get you to verify using your phone number. If we refuse to let the application find our friends and acquaintances or to show our number publicly, we still inexplicably end up in the recommended friends lists of people we know. Unlike other social media users, we are forced to be invested in our privacy to an extent that we can't possibly ignore this or forget about it. Seeing a suggestion to add a family member or work colleague as a friend on an account featuring nude photos and escorting advertisements has struck fear into the hearts of too many sex workers to count. If we're getting the recommendation… so are they.

On top of using a different device and number, sex workers also avoid surveillance by using e-mail services like Proton Mail which have end-to-end encryption. Other e-mail providers track online behaviour, largely for the purpose of advertising, and that's a sex worker's worst nightmare. If we're taking booking through our e-mail as well as using it to sign up to escorting websites, we also have to worry about protecting ourselves against further tracking through spy pixels that could be sent to us by our clients. All of our online activity is impacted by our need to dodge the constant attempts made by individuals and companies and the police to monitor us.

Online surveillance of sex workers has become increasingly popular, but that does not mean that physical surveillance of us has lessened. Street and brothel workers, some of whom bypass the need to advertise online at all because they rely on their location as a form of advertising or are managed by third parties, are the most at risk when it comes to this kind of physical surveillance.

From the warmth of their vehicles and paid at tax-payers' expense, police watch street sex workers in areas they are already known to work. In the UK, their word alone allows them to give out Prostitute's Cautions to anyone they spot on the street who they believe is a sex worker. These cautions cannot be appealed and show up on enhanced DBS checks for 100 years. In countries where the sale of sex is illegal, police frequently arrest those they believe are street sex workers for soliciting. In countries where the sale of sex is highly regulated, street sex workers are watched by police who check whether they are licensed and they harass and arrest those who are not or who are working in areas that regulations forbid.

Hooker Mentality

Not all surveillance of street sex workers ends in arrest. Police also leverage their knowledge of sex workers' working patterns to assault them, threatening fines or arrest if they don't provide their sexual services to them for free. Street-based workers are highly vulnerable to this kind of targetting because their ability to earn a living relies on the streets they work on becoming well-known for prostitution. Making sure clients have this knowledge means advertising their presence enough that locals and eventually the police take notice too. If they report an officer who abuses them, they are likely to be protected by their friends on the force and the sex worker will rarely see any kind of justice.

Brothel workers face a similar problem because of the static nature of their venues. Review forums fill up with clients talking about visiting known walk-in venues or massage parlours where it's an open secret that people can pay for sex by the hour. Less traditional brothels where multiple people work from the same flat but don't advertise that way can still be uncovered by clients who use online message boards to discuss the locations of the sex workers they've met. The police use this information, as well as cross-referencing the pictures in escorts' profiles on advertising websites to see if we're using the same houses and flats, as a way to track brothel workers. Some police operations involve posing as clients via text to obtain postcodes and full addresses where possible to get an even better idea of which sex workers might be working together.

Raids can be arranged on these brothels, leading to strip searches of the inhabitants and highly personal questions being asked. Depending on the law where these raids occur, sex workers might be arrested en masse or classed as potential victims. If these raids reveal enough foreign sex workers they can swiftly turn into immigration raids. Rarely do these invasions disrupt anyone but sex workers ourselves, ending in deportations of immigrant workers and a loss of income for those who are citizens even when they are not arrested. Workers might be labelled as complicit in the running of the establishment or threatened with brothel management charges to bully them into admitting who runs the place. These raids violate privacy on a multitude of levels, with officers rifling through bags and visually inspecting workers after making them undress, only to receive praise from news outlets about cracking down on pimps and traffickers.

Using similar tactics to those employed to find the locations of brothels, police in the UK also ascertain who to target for what they call "welfare checks". The intent of these checks is not to criminalize us quite yet, but to let us know they are watching. Claims to want to ensure we are not being coerced and to offer help are made, with the full knowledge that the police are the last people most hookers want to go to in that situation, as the most common kind of excuse. Justifications range

110

from a sex worker looking sad in their pictures to reviews claiming they were nervous, as well as other factors like frequent changes in postcode and rates that are on the lower end of the spectrum. Anything we do can be cited as a cause for concern.

The typical way that an independent sex worker will end up meeting a police officer for their welfare check is through subterfuge. An officer will pose as a client over the phone or through text messages, show up in plain clothes so he doesn't look suspicious if the sex worker gets eyes on him before he's through the door, and he'll reveal himself once they're alone inside the bedroom. This officer will almost exclusively be male because of the typical gender demographics of clients, so as not to arouse suspicion, with the people they're "checking on" mostly being women.

I experienced a welfare check by a police officer whilst I was fairly new to brothel work. I was 19, finally settling into the routine of meeting with clients from the flat, and I was having a slow night. A client inquiry came in and the anonymous man asked me if he could make an immediate booking. I gave him the postcode immediately and waited for him. He arrived 45 minutes later and was one of the few clients I'd had at that location who appeared not to struggle with following my instructions reaching the flat as I guided him while watching his grainy image on the CCTV. In hindsight, that should have been a red flag.

Hooker Mentality

Once the client was inside, I walked him down the hall to the bedroom where I planned to follow my usual procedure. I would ask him for the money upfront and hide it away in a coffee tin in the living room before we got started. I distinctly remember that he put his hand on my lower back which was bare in the cut-out dress I was wearing at the time. When we reached the room, he kept asking questions about how long I'd been working from the flat I was in and how many others worked there too. I knew enough to refuse to answer. Only after I got firm with him about paying did he reveal that he was a police officer and my blood went ice cold. I was suddenly dunked into a high-pressure situation where saying the wrong thing might result in my place of work being shut down. I really needed the money to save enough to pay 6 months rent on the new flat I was moving into soon. The last thing on my mind was complaining about mistreatment from the brothel manager, because I knew it wouldn't benefit me.

Starting these check-ins with deception is not the sort of thing you'd expect from people who want to protect us. It creates a situation where the person being checked on is surprised, scared, and has lost out on money from the booking they would have had during that time slot if they'd gotten a real client. I've never heard of a police officer handing over the money that was agreed upon in advance. These unannounced visits are disruptive, intimidating, and seem to have ulterior motives. SCOT-PEP, a sex worker-led charity advocating for our rights and safety, noted this back in 2016 with regards to Police Scotland's SHAW (support, health and wellbeing) visits to people selling sex:

"We have now seen that part of Police Scotland's own remit with regards to Operation SHAW is to 'identify other criminality'. For sex workers in our network, this raises the frightening possibility that Police Scotland are conducting surveillance and surprise home visits on sex workers under the veneer of offering 'help and support', while in fact looking for opportunities to criminalise sex workers for drug use, immigration offences or anything else they can find."[ix]

In spite of what the state would like to have us believe, the police do not have eyes and ears everywhere. Expanding their reach and the extent of their surveillance to places they are not regularly stationed requires more than a few welfare checks targetting vulnerable people. Police also rely heavily on recruiting ordinary working class people as unwitting spies, saving them the man-hours and resources needed to send officers into people's homes and workplaces. Hospitality workers, particularly those who work in the hotels where sex workers who take outcalls meet with our clients, are a particularly desirable group to conscript for this purpose.

Hotel employees are convinced to become extra eyes and ears for the police regarding the whereabouts of sex workers through propaganda fed to them in their workplace training. They are told to look out for signs of human trafficking and report to their managers if they see any, which are in turn shared with the police if the manager thinks the evidence is sufficient. To gather more info, these managers might harass guests they assume are sex workers, call up to their room, or as friends of mine have experienced they might even enter the room without permission. Key-carded hotels are my personal nightmare because they make it so much harder to avoid the receptions-turned-spies.

Surveillance of hookers is also commonly outsourced to residents of areas with a high prevalence of sex work, particularly with street sex work. This brings the amount of harassment levelled against sex workers to a peak, due to the constant close proximity to their tormentors, and leaves them no recourse to hide from the violation of their privacy. Residents aren't limited to police working hours, nor are they bound by an expectation not to make a public fuss which will result in negative PR. The police are able to use them to secure outcomes they desire but cannot publicly admit to wanting without looking comically evil. Intimidation tactics are combined with surveillance.

In Holbeck (Leeds, UK), residents were used to collect information about sex workers in the Managed Zone where police had effectively decriminalized street prostitution inside of a small area in 2014. The idea was that this managed approach to the sale of sex would be a

114

test run, permitting public solicitation only during set hours and on specific roads, as a way to assess the utility of a different legal model. Naturally, what the police actually wanted was for this managed approach to fail. They stationed a small number of officers in the Managed Zone to watch over it and stoked the flames of disapproval from a small number of locals until they had protests and constant complaints on their hands.

The independent review of the managed approach which ultimately resulted in the end of it struggled to get these resident responses. There was so much apathy, barring small groups of locals who strongly opposed prostitution and had extremely classist attitudes towards visibly poor and struggling residents, that they resorted to multiple methods to find respondents. Researchers conducted a residents survey which was advertised by leafleting 1940 residences, however the response rate was so low that they quickly resorted to posting in local Facebook groups and personally walking residents through how to take part. In total, they managed to get only 120 people (covering 6% of eligible households) to complete the survey[x]. This exemplifies how when people aren't naturally inclined to spy on their neighbours, pressure can be applied until some do and the state gets its way.

Our distrust of police doesn't stop sex workers from succumbing to these pressures in all cases either. We are susceptible to being exploited by police as an unpaid labour force of informants with the right incentive. One of the most compelling motivations they manipulate us with is the chance to protect children from sexual exploitation. These kinds of operations are sold to the public as heart-warming tales of sex workers as unlikely protectors. Project Night Light in Bristol works this way, with the explicit purpose of identifying vulnerable under-18s being targeted by the clients of street sex workers. In reality, initiatives like this put these same workers in more danger by pressuring them into continuing to see their worst clients to gather information.

One of the sex workers approached by the Night Light team, given the pseudonym Anna in public coverage, made this explicit when she expressed that she kept seeing a client who sickened her specifically because she felt obligated to get this information to the police[xi]. Anna was not compensated for this work and was ultimately put at a much higher personal risk as a result. That's without even mentioning the toll on her mental health.

"On one occasion a man, who was paying her for sex, asked her to engage in role-play, where she had to pretend to be a primary school age girl.

"It was really unpleasant. Sickening to be honest," she said. "I had to carry on for three months, but I couldn't walk away until I knew what was happening."

Hooker Mentality

After reporting her concerns to the police, it turned out the man was abusing his eight-year-old daughter. 'Anna' gave evidence, and he was sent to prison.

"If you think there's a chance you're leaving a child in that position, you've got to stay. You've got to find out," she said."

For many sex workers who have experienced repeated abuse from our youth until adulthood, both in and out of prostitution, assaults are something we have come to accept as part of our lives. The idea of making sacrifices to be close to clients who harm us so that we can protect young people who have not yet been subject to it, or who have begun being assaulted but are in a position where they may be helped before it becomes a repeated and life-long issue, feels like a noble goal. I have felt this way myself when swallowing my urge to vomit so that I could act sweet towards a regular client who detailed to me the abuse he was enacting on various young girls, just to get the contact information of these girls and support them to escape from him when I was only a teenager myself. Unfortunately schemes like this don't do what they promise, even for those of us who would be willing to make the trade.

Other types of surveillance happen without police encouragement, or whilst disguising it, by people who claim to seek to support us. Behind the scenes, they are sharing our personal data with the government in their reporting. They may or may not be entirely forthcoming about that. Many of these people are well-meaning, working as part of support services and charities which use their funding to provide us with STI testing and safer sex supplies, however over the course of doing this work they collect information about us. The data might come in the form of stating how many people they recorded as having reactive HIV tests or the total number of sex workers who attended one of their drop-ins, though ultimately the result is always that reports are made and the state gains access to the information.

When we manage to fly under the radar and protect our identities from all of these groups, our security still risks being compromised. It gets weaker the more well-known we become. This can happen through becoming known to our local police who may target us personally for monitoring, as well as being the result of rising online popularity. We're one viral advertisement away from being outed and banned from multiple countries, in addition to the risk that we will be disowned by our families and fired from our jobs upon discovery.

Articles written about sex workers are one way we might obtain a dangerous level of notoriety outside of the area we live in. Activists frequently use false names when speaking about our experiences selling sex, avoiding the inclusion of pictures at all, but any sex worker who agrees to speak to a journalist is taking a huge risk. Highly motivated writers who want a sensational story might dig into our backgrounds and uncover information we had no idea was accessible, making us vulnerable, and they almost never do their due diligence to check that their subjects are comfortable with what will be shared.

Journalists frequently seek out sex workers who have minimal experience with being interviewed and have no idea how large the public reaction will be, because more seasoned communicators on the topic of sex workers' rights will not allow themselves to be taken advantage of. Under the excuse of journalistic ethics around not wanting to sway what interviewees might say, sex workers are not paid for our expertise and often spend more time explaining basic concepts to the person writing about our community than we do actually giving our perspective. When these articles are released, they often include contrasting positions from those who want to deny us rights as workers, framing radical feminists and conservatives as objective while twisting our words and focusing on our trauma. We are not only monitored and investigated for these pieces in newspapers or magazines serve; we are used for propaganda against our own interests.

To make anti sex worker propaganda extra effective towards the average person, more surveillance is required to produce statistics that can be referred back to. Researchers seek out sex workers, individually and in groups, for the purpose of gathering this data. One could be forgiven for believing their claims to want to understand how widespread our issues are as a prelude to resolving them, but the unfortunate reality is that data gathered about our suffering is typically used to argue our industry must be abolished. Inevitably, activism for the abolition of prostitution leaves us with worse outcomes.

Observing sex workers and surveying or interviewing us for the purpose of creating statistics on the amount of violence we experience is made all the more difficult for researchers because we're encouraged to actively avoid them for self-preservation. The sex workers who will speak to these researchers are usually those who sell sex in such chaotic scenarios and with such little support that they cannot hide and have little left to lose, or the most privileged who have the time and resources to protect their identities and avoid criminalization. Those who cannot avoid surveillance have no choice but to comply with being watched in the hopes of any help upon the reveal of their suffering.

A full understanding of the extent of the problem with how researches monitor their subjects requires that we break down some studies. These are meant to exemplify the issue and show the extent of the problem, not to be an exhaustive list or a showcase of the most popularly cited studies:

Prostitution and Trafficking in Nine Countries: An Update on Violence and Post-Traumatic Stress Disorder[xii].

In this study, researchers interviewed 854 people across 9 countries. From the creation of statistics based on these findings which speak about sex work in a generalized way, a claim is implied that the results can be generalized to prostitution as a whole.

"We found that prostitution was multitraumatic: 71% were physically assaulted in prostitution; 63% were raped; 89% of these respondents wanted to escape prostitution, but did not have other options for survival. A total of 75% had been homeless at some point in their lives; 68% met criteria for PTSD."

Our first major red flag for this study is the way the countries included (Canada, Colombia, Germany, Mexico, USA, Thailand, Zambia, Turkey, South Africa) were chosen. There were selected "because investigators in those states shared a commitment to documenting the experiences of women in prostitution", which introduces a significant selection bias based on where the most surveillance is already happening and who is doing it. Nothing is done to mitigate the possibility that heightened observation and documentation itself could impact sex workers' experiences.

Of the 854 interviewees, 100 were sex workers interviewed in Canada from *"in or near Vancouver's Downtown Eastside, one of the most economic destitute regions in North America"*. This is nothing close to a representative sampling of Canadian sex workers. 123 were from two different cities in Mexico, though we have no information about how they were chosen. 54 sex workers from Hamburg in Germany were interviewed, chosen from shelters for "drug addicted women" and from vocational rehabilitation programs for sex workers and those who responded to local newspaper ads. 130 street sex workers were interviewed in San Francisco. 110 interviewees came from Thailand, mostly found through an agency offering job training and working on the streets or from a beauty parlour. 68 were from South African brothels, streets, and a drop-in centre. 117 were interviewed in Zambia through TASINTHA, an organisation supporting sex workers with food and vocational training. 50 interviewees were found in Turkey, all from those "who were brought to a hospital in Istanbul by police for the purpose of STD control." 96 sex workers were interviewed in Columbia, all from agencies.

From these interviews, a claim is made about the findings. *"Our findings contradict common myths about prostitution: the assumption that street prostitution is the worst type of prostitution, that prostitution of men and boys is different from prostitution of women and girls, that most of those in prostitution freely consent to it, that most people are in prostitution because of drug addiction, that prostitution is qualitatively different from trafficking, and that legalizing or decriminalizing prostitution would decrease its harm."*

These claims are not sufficiently supported by the data collected, because the sex workers they were able to interview were the most marginalized and controlled by design. The sex workers who were forced into a hospital in Istanbul for STI control had no choice in being watched, turning them into convenient participants who came from backgrounds where they were far more likely to have been subject to abuse. Pulling so many subjects from agencies increased the likelihood of abuse because of the lack of autonomy the workers were given and poor working conditions. Anyone accessing support services to stop selling sex or cease using drugs would be selling sex in especially difficult circumstances too, their troubles being exactly what led them into the researchers hands.

A truly representative sample would include people selling sex in managed and independent scenarios in venues and on the street within each country, in proportion with their prevalence. That isn't information the researchers had, since their surveillance network was largely made up of support services and fellow researchers observing street workers, so they rely on the ignorance of the average person to launder the results of their study.

Screening for Traumatic Brain Injury in Prostituted Women[xiii]

Hooker Mentality

In this study of only 66 participants, all clients of agencies offering services to women "escaping prostitution" in San Francisco, Chicago, and Toronto, any broad statistical relevance of the data is undermined by choosing exclusively women who want to stop selling sex. Of those who were questioned on whether they had a history of head injuries as part of these focus groups, 60 had a lifetime history of one and 40 had sustained at least one whilst selling sex. No clarification is provided as to whether these head injuries were the result of abuse by clients and third parties controlling them, or if they simply occurred during the same time period that these women were selling sex at the hands of intimate partners or acquaintances.

High rates of TBIs are expected among women who have experienced abuse and abuse is generally hidden by perpetrators and victims alike. It is the poorest and most vulnerable who have no choice but to access free services when the abuse gets too severe to cope with, and they are the ones who end up being asked questions about incidences of head injuries. This kind of common sense conclusion is often evident to researchers, yet not to the larger institutions or those opposed to sex work who cite their findings.

What this kind of research shows us is that sex workers cannot win when it comes to having our lives studied, only mitigate harm. We do our best to avoid being counted and having our lives picked apart to be written down and we succeed in doing so most often when we are in more advantageous positions. There will always be people who do not have the means to protect themselves or who will agree to an interview for some cash, largely our most vulnerable, and their experiences will be noted down and generalized to us all. On the other end of the spectrum we have a small number of the most privileged hookers who are willing to be observed, whom governments and private individuals alike find it very easy to dismiss as the outliers they are.

An unfortunate side-effect of sex workers' avoidance of surveillance is that when researchers cannot find enough real people to generate an answer they will simply make up the data. This made up data cannot easily be contradicted, no matter how easy it is to prove it's no better than a guess, and in the absence of anything better many groups would rather quote false numbers than go without. We can see this especially with regards to the desire to state a total number of sex workers in a given region.

The Office for National Statistics commissioned a report in 2015[xiv] in the hopes of getting a figure for the number of sex workers in the UK and the size of our economic activity. They came up against the exact issues you'd expect. A total of 72,816 sex workers was estimated based on the number who access support services. They took the average number of clients helped by the sex worker support services they contacted and then multiplied it by the total number of services. Only a fraction of active sex workers will use support services and we're concentrated in areas where work is most lucrative instead of being evenly dispersed. I can confidently state that their calculation provides a massive underestimate.

The Home Office later commissioned a report[xv], which came out in October 2019, containing a number of these flawed estimates of the UK sex worker population size. Thankfully, this report actually acknowledged how far off these figures were likely to be. One estimate from Kinnell in 1999 suggested there were 80,000 of us, based on what employees of sex worker support services believed. Another, from 2017, estimated 104,946 based on the number of people advertising on a single online platform. No attempts were made to account for the number of people trading or selling sex informally on a short-term basis, nor did any of the figures try to account for other kinds of sex workers who might avoid support services such as migrants concerned about being deported or more privileged workers who have little reason to need them.

Whatever the total number actually is doesn't honestly matter to the state in any country. What matters is whether the number can be used to justify further surveillance. If they claim there are 100,000 sex workers in the UK, the UK government can justify spending enough money to repress and monitor that many sex workers. From there, if they can generate a percentage for how many workers are trafficked or experience violence, they can get themselves a new number that allows for specific kinds of intervention claiming to protect those subject to harm. Members of Parliament seem to have a particular interest in using these numbers to treat any anti sex work policy as a VAWG (violence against women and girls) counter-measure.

There's no way to get accurate totals on the number of sex workers subjected to violence anywhere. Research into small groups of sex workers can't be generalized to us all and no government records whether someone's a sex worker when they're murdered or assaulted as a standard practice. The police don't want to admit how badly they are failing us, so we rely on sex worker-led organisations to record names and numbers based on news stories and members of their community who are known to have been killed. Isolated sex workers die and their names never make it onto these lists of our dead. For this reason, the recorded sex worker murder rates will never be anywhere close to real numbers.

National Ugly Mugs (a UK-based organisation committed to ending violence against sex workers) keeps track of sex workers murdered in the UK since 1990.[xvi] As of International Day to End Violence Against Sex Workers in 2024, this list contained 199 sex workers. They rightfully acknowledge that their list is not exhaustive because not all names have been made public and some victims were not open about their work. Some simply wouldn't have wanted their names to be included and groups like NUM respect that. This list exists so that we can mourn those we know about, as we keep in mind the others we have known personally or whose deaths have been swept under the rug.

Assault rates also go under-reported because sex workers are well aware that the police are not our friends. To seek legal recourse against our attackers we're forced to announce our profession to the same cops who are more likely to mock us than offer genuine empathy and care in the aftermath of a rape or other physical attack. Though politicians and people who don't trust sex workers to tell the truth might prefer to get their numbers through official channels, the best way to get a sense of the frequency of abuse (if not murder) is to survey sex workers ourselves. A representative sample is hard to find, so the resulting statistics can't be relied upon to be perfectly accurate, but this gives us a sense of scale.

To further understand when there has been an increase in violence against sex workers, regardless of whether the amount recorded is exact, we need to make comparisons within the same context where other factors remain static. A report on the introduction of the Nordic Model to France in April 2016 does this, looking at the number of murders and the amount of violence that sex workers self-reported before and after the introduction of the law. It is noted by the authors that the word of sex workers is almost never considered to be a valuable source of evidence no matter the manner it is collected in. In one study cited, 42.3% of sex workers said they experienced more violence than before the legal change. In another, it is noted that 41 Chinese sex workers in Paris reported being victimized between April and September before the new law was introduced and that 71 reported being victimized during the same time frame afterwards[xvii]. The data collection still isn't perfect – its consistency simply allows us to see the pattern.

Politicians and pressure groups who oppose sex workers' rights often pull up the misleading statistics they can find about assaults and murders of sex workers, all using different methods for their estimations, and find ways to compare them to support conclusions they've already decided upon. They'll say twice as many sex workers were murdered in a country with legal or decriminalised sex work compared to one with the Nordic model and use this to argue that criminalizing clients is safer. Even when non sex workers know these numbers are inaccurate or look into the sources and find them lacking, they have no sense of how far off these numbers are. Sex workers can have an incredibly different experience because we might personally know more sex workers who were assaulted, killed or went missing that year than the total number recorded.

Sex workers are also primed to question where these numbers come from when we're well aware that our own assaults haven't been recorded anywhere. I reported being raped by a client only once and learned that it was worse to suffer through police interrogation about the assault than to say nothing, especially given the incredibly low conviction rate and my certainty that sending my abuser to prison would have done no good regardless. I never considered reporting any of the physical and sexual assaults I have been subjected to since, which must be in the dozens. Knowing that my own incidents of being assaulted aren't being included in the statistics prompts me to wonder how many orders of magnitude they might be off by.

Juxtaposing the extreme surveillance sex workers experience with the underground nature of our work that encourages large swathes of us evade detection, we end up with a conclusion that makes very little sense to people who aren't used to living in the metaphorical panopticon: trying to watch us more closely leads to a more inaccurate picture. Their attempts to zoom in leave us pixelated on a screen to the point of being unrecognizable. Hookers know we're being watched and that those observations will still manage to get so many things wrong.

Chapter 6:
Police and Prison Abolition

Criminalization has come nowhere near getting rid of sex workers. We are notoriously subject to extreme levels of policing and we are still everywhere. Police officers find themselves among our worst clients and our tormentors, both on and off-duty. We are allowed to exist under the thumb of the state to the extent that we benefit them or aren't worth their time to police. At the same time, they make sure we are never permitted to thrive.

Hating the police and being a police abolitionist go hand in hand, but one does not automatically lead to the other in all cases. To make the leap, we have to understand that the police are a group designed to beat the populace into submission in line with the state's interests, rather than focusing solely on the ways they make our lives worse as individuals. There are no good cops; every single one is complicit by taking the job. Sex workers can often fall into the trap of believing that

131

our oppression at the hands of these cops is our own fault for engaging in an immoral practice, or that we are collateral damage in a system designed to protect people which can be tweaked and reformed, because we are brainwashed to agree with the interests of the state. This manipulation is exposed for what it is, to those willing to see it, when we consider how much more harshly sex workers are targeted than perpetrators of sexual violence. You can't sell sex for long without being made viscerally aware of this fact.

Conviction rates of rapists vary wildly by country and time period. Across the board, only a small portion of those who are reported end up being charged and found guilty. Rape cases also take a disproportionate length of time to investigate compared to many other crimes, with part of the excuse for this being that the systems claiming to be aiming for justice are too overwhelmed by the sheer volume. Low rates of reporting by victims are no surprise under these conditions. Add in someone being a sex worker and we see even worse outcomes, with victims being mistreated or harassed by the same police who promise to help them. Our professions are then recorded, meaning that future cops will know we're sex workers by looking at our file when we face any further legal issues, compounding our suffering.

There is no version of a police force that would be good for sex workers because there is no version of the police which does not utilize their power to enact the will of the state through a monopoly on violence. Watching other sex workers rarely get their rapists convicted, meanwhile dealing with the daily repercussions of being criminalized for a job which does no harm, forces many of us to accept that the police are no kind of fallback whether we share that broader understanding or not. We must have the right to defend ourselves and to seek the support of our community to defend us, rather than being expected to rely on an outside force to arbitrate and enact punishment as they see fit. Punishment and the threat of it does not deter our abusers.

People who rape sex workers get away with doing so and others do even worse; serial killers choose sex workers as targets because we're so devalued that police won't investigate our deaths thoroughly. Dead hookers are the butt of jokes. We know of a few killers who exemplify the problem, but part of what terrifies sex workers so much is the number of our killers who will never be caught. Our friends go missing and we never get answers.

Those who knew and loved the victims of Samuel Little didn't get their own closure until 2014 when he was convicted of several murders and admitted to a total of 93 shortly after. Based purely on the murders he confessed to which were able to be confirmed, Little was labelled the most prolific serial killer in US history for the lives he took between 1970 and 2005. The reason he was ultimately caught wasn't even because the police were actually looking into the murders – it was a drug charge where his DNA was taken. The majority of his victims were sex workers and/or homeless women precisely because he believed he could get away with killing them for longer. He was right.

Although Little was the most prolific killer of sex workers caught in the US, he was far from the first and certainly not the only one. Across the world, sex workers are targets. There are widely known figures like Jack the Ripper and his more recent namesake the Yorkshire Ripper, then other killers whose names aren't well-known but who exclusively targeted sex workers like Steven Wright and David Smith. There are yet more killers who included sex workers among their victims opportunistically, like Jeffrey Dahmer. These are the kinds of predators who cause hookers to tell our friends what address we're going to for a booking or to take a picture of a client's license plate. We don't imagine we can escape if such a killer comes after us; these precautions exist as a desperate attempt to leave as much evidence behind as possible so that a Steven Wright doesn't avoid capture long enough to become a Samuel Little.

This attitude that the police have of brushing it off when sex workers die and not thoroughly investigating doesn't apply in reverse. The double standard is no clearer than in cases where people who have sold sex (of their own volition or under threat) are punished for killing their abusers in self-defence. Chrystul Kizer and

Cyntoia Brown are two examples that stand out to me. They are both women who killed the men who trafficked them for sex when they were still minors, after the police repeatedly failed to protect them. Vigilantism is condemned while the system shows an undeniable bias against sex workers, leaving us no choice other than to use violence ourselves rather than wait fruitlessly for the police to do so with state approval. Once we do, we're punished.

Aileen Wuornos was a rare exception to the general rule that predators get to murder sex workers and we don't get to enact violence in return. Her ability to kill the clients who attempted to rape her, for which she was ultimately given the death penalty, was dependent on the police allowing it until they saw fit to intervene. Aileen herself noted this in an interview close to the end of her life, *"I'd shoot, shoot the guy if I ran into trouble, physical trouble, the cops knew it. When the physical trouble came along, let her clean the streets, and then we'll pull her in. That's why."*[xviii] Police were able to find tax funded man-hours to stalk street sex workers like Aileen, yet there was never enough money around to help her. She was used as a tool by the police to deal with abusers who caused a public nuisance, only to be punished for doing what they pushed her into once she'd done it.

From every angle, it is clear that the police view sex workers' lives as disposable. Politicians are no better. Members of parliament and senators with the power to support our plight will book time with sex workers and still seek to put us in prison or fine us for doing the very things they demand. They claim to want us gone while fucking us behind closed doors. This isn't evidence of a contradiction in beliefs – it is a calculated set of lies to obtain their true goal. Through criminalizing us, they restrict our ability to find clients and leave us at their mercy. If one of their favourite hookers gets snatched up by the law, they can quickly be replaced. They can either pay off a few corrupt cops or wait for another worker to fill the void who will likely be marginalized and poor and receptive to whatever their demands are. Cycling through hookers keeps our desperation high and our prices low. For every sex worker thrown in prison there is another person on the cusp of starting, one unpaid bill away from putting up an online advertisement or signing up to an agency and totally naïve.

Within prisons, prostitution continues. Pressures to trade sex only increase in positions of precarity and resources in prison are so scarce. Prisoners lack access to money unless they went into the prison system wealthy or they have people on the outside looking out for them and topping up their accounts. They're also frequently in physical danger that they may want to trade to protect themselves from, while lacking material goods of value to do so with. It's a perfect environment for creating hookers out of people who wouldn't otherwise have sold sex, in addition to encouraging current sex workers to continue.

The people who are most capable of offering or rescinding types of protection, who also have the easiest access to contraband that incarcerated people want to trade for, are guards. These guards have so much power over prisoners that they often don't need to put in effort to extort them. Inmates will already feel compelled to agree to sex because of the implicit threat that life will be made harder for them if they refuse. Some of the people agreeing to these trades will have done sex work before, as people arrested on prostitution-related charges will be more likely to be approached, but ultimately these pressures will work on almost anyone.

Among prisoners themselves, access to mutually enjoyable sex is limited due to the gender segregation of facilities and the fact most inmates are straight. For those willing to be "gay for the stay" despite their lack of attraction, purchasing sexual favours seems an obvious way to ensure their position as the active partner. If an inmate is in need of money, providing those sex acts as the receptive party becomes an equally obvious solution. These dynamics occur in both men's and women's prisons, however the sexual economy in men's prisons and the frequency of rape there is far more notorious.

Trans women inmates face some of the harshest pressures when held in men's prisons. Sarah Jane Baker, Britain's longest-serving trans inmate, has spoken about trading sex in prison at length and her observations of other trans women doing the same. She wrote:

> *"Whenever I or my trans-sisters were offered the opportunity to come out of our protection cells, men would come on to us, trying to catch our attention. We would be offered drugs, the use of mobile phones or a shoulder to cry on."[xix]*

Combining this with the common requests she received for sexual domination, where *"men would pay [her] copious amounts of drugs to tie them up and humiliate them"*, this establishes a pattern of incarcerated men bartering the few possessions they can obtain for sex. Insidiously, I have learned from many previously incarcerated trans women that the "opportunity" to leave these protection cells or isolation is often given with the express intent of seeing them abused by the cis men in the general prison population.

In women's prisons, a large proportion of inmates have traded sex in the past whether or not that is the reason for their current incarceration. In the US this can often be upwards of 30% of all of the women who are currently detained in an area[xx]. People who aim to target vulnerable women and earn money from their work selling sex know this and find it far more profitable to target people who are already used to selling sex than to groom new people into the profession. Without other ways to earn money upon being released from prison, they accept offers from pimps who approach them or continue to work independently until they are caught again and returned to prison. This creates a cycle which is only sometimes interrupted during their time spent in prison. Of course for many sex workers of all genders, trading sex doesn't stop during those periods of incarceration at all.

Prostitution being so commonplace in one of the most strictly monitored places a person can live tells us that no amount of surveillance will stop people from selling or trading sex when the need is great enough. The failure of the prison system to protect inmates from guards, other incarcerated people, or predators waiting outside of the grounds further demonstrates that they don't even care to stop us. They let pimps prey upon those being released to get them to sell more sex and wait until the same people end up being returned to prison. Recidivism is almost guaranteed in these circumstances. With that in mind, it is clearly a foolish claim that greater police surveillance of areas with a high rate of prostitution will lead to less of it. Criminalization will not put an end to sex work because *it doesn't actually seek to.*

Supposed police and prison abolitionists may still struggle with this truth about the actual goals of a police force. They often have a very flimsy commitment to the ideology if they're not regularly at high risk of arrest and were raised with the expectation that the police are the right group to call in an emergency. The police are perceived as a threat to others rather than to them. Minor inconveniences and paranoia can lead these pseudo-abolitionists to picking up the phone and calling the emergency line. Most sex workers are not afforded the luxury of being believed or supported by police, so we don't need to read abolitionist texts on a regular basis to renew our commitment (although it admittedly helps with deeper understanding). Our abolitionist positions are deeply held and informed by our interactions with the police and prisons. Therefore they hold up to situations which are far more extreme.

Otherwise progressive people often talk themselves into following along with the status quo and call the police to soothe their nerves or for their own convenience. I've seen a woman who calls herself an anarchist call the cops over a man sitting in his car for a few hours while parked across the road from her house, all because he unsettled her. Past friends who've ranted alongside me about the dangers of proximity to law enforcement have called them over a stolen bike. On one occasion, several members of a local communist group suggested informing the police of the location of their next planned protest with the hopes they'd send chaperones while I watched in dismay. Meanwhile, hookers I know have been avoiding police like the plague.

A large proportion of the hookers I know have the first instinct to call a friend rather than the police in situations of physical danger, let alone those of mild discomfort or where there's only a potential threat. I've gotten calls to meet friends in the aftermath of assaults to take care of them without a whiff of a desire to call the police. I've called my co-workers and the brothel manager when a group of men were trying to break down the door of the brothel I was working in, the idea of calling the cops never entering my mind. Dozens of brothel workers I've known have had money go missing on shift and their solution has been to handle it interpersonally. Rather than relying on the state's monopoly on violence, hookers will go as far as breaking the law themselves to handle these problems with a variety of methods ranging from theft to manipulation to physical self-defence that we know wouldn't hold up in a court room.

Calling the police on an abusive partner who won't return the passport of the sex worker they're dating, holding it over them to control their work, could result in the arrest of the victim just as easily as the perpetrator. Alternatively, calling friends to intimidate that partner into giving it up or breaking in and stealing it is a solution which results in none of those harms. We can spread out the risk of injury and retaliation by working in groups and being as covert as possible with our aims. Taking matters into our own hands without an impartial third party isn't the ideal solution, but the police aren't impartial either. The jump from our hands-on approach to conflict and harm to a restorative justice model is not such a chasm as it is between the restorative ideal and a carceral approach.

The struggle to get this mindset to spread can be linked to the necessity of keeping it quiet for the people who are marginalized enough to develop it. Talking about these behaviours openly makes me break out into a cold sweat. Anyone without such constant repeated lessons on not trusting the police can easily be persuaded by the copaganda around them to rat us out the second things get tough, repeating what we say to the same police who terrorize us. Only in hindsight, years after the events, can some of our systems for self-protection come to light without compromising the safety of those involved.

When sex workers would like to call for help from outside of the community, the police are typically an active hindrance. Each time I am with a frail elderly client or one who has serious health issues, I worry acutely about what I would do for this reason. Horror stories of sex workers whose clients have had heart attacks in a room at the brothel play through my mind as sweat drips onto me from a man I know has taken far too much Viagra to be safe. I've workshopped plans for these eventualities with other workers more times than I can count. If he were able to walk, I could guide him down the road and call 999 claiming to have found him collapsed on the street complaining of chest pains. If he were unconscious, I could recruit help to carry him outside while a maid called and said she spotted him through the window. We could take a taxi to the hospital if one is close enough, where I would leave him when we reached the doors of the emergency room. Luckily I've never had to face this eventuality, however there are many sex workers who've had to weigh up the harm police might do to them and their client compared to the risk to life from whatever health issue crops up.

The more criminalized sex work is, the more difficult these choices become. Is it worth prison time to buy a client you probably don't even like an extra minute to get treatment for a stroke? Are we ethically obligated to make that trade no matter the unfairness of it? Regardless of where a sex worker falls on answering these questions, it is clear to us all that it's an unreasonable situation for us to be placed in that we never asked for. Without the police as a factor, we would be free to do what is in the best interests of the client's health instead of weighing it up against our own.

Knowing the police are not only useless but actively detrimental puts sex workers in the right frame of mind to hear "police and prison abolition" without jumping to the question of what we do about violence. We can picture a future where we work together to determine what is best for the collective, safeguarding victims according to their actual wants and needs rather than antiquated laws that serve the interests of a government. Questions of what happens to rapists in a world without police have an easy answer – *more than happens to them now.*

Hooker Mentality

It's not a hard sell to get hookers on board with an end to policing and incarceration. What can be hard is getting us to visualize a world where the communities we form beyond other sex workers would have our backs, to do better than just getting rid of a problematic structure. I want to enable sex workers to imagine a future where we form a society that is capable of rehabilitation and protection of the vulnerable in the way we are falsely promised the police will. To make this happen, we need real allies who won't fold the second things get tough.

Chapter 7:
Borders, Immigration and Trafficking

Human trafficking is rampant in a number of industries, driven by poor economic circumstances. Exceptionalism about sexual labour and irrational white supremacist fears about the corruption of white women have lead to a sex trafficking panic which eclipses concerns about other kinds of trafficking within the public discourse in the West. Heedless of the unconscionable underpayment and forced labour experienced by immigrants working in agriculture, domestic servitude and construction, media urges us to focus on the boogeyman of a pimp snatching women off of the street to become sex slaves.

All kinds of human trafficking have similar root causes of financial need combined with an unequal distribution of wealth between countries and classes. Closed borders and strict immigration requirements make up the other piece of the puzzle that gives traffickers power over their victims. Disadvantaged people understandably want to work in countries where their labour is valued more highly and the standard of living is better, thus they are easy targets for smugglers of people. Some of these exploiters will lie about the conditions workers will be met with, but I would be remiss not to mention the scenarios where traffickers are mostly honest and their targets have no better options. Whether the plan is to work off an inflated debt to the traffickers before seeking out independent work or to serve them indefinitely, trafficking is an affront to our dignity which is enabled by restrictions on human movement.

Anyone can come to these conclusions by talking to victims of this kind of trafficking. Sex workers are uniquely catalysed into considering the topic by the fact that our work is often considered to be trafficking by default. I've been stopped at the border and interrogated about my history and the possibility a client or pimp was coercing me into taking a flight, purely because I placed my own advert on an escorting site. Border control officers assuming independent sex workers must be under the influence of a third party when we're touring or going on holiday forces us to ask how often such false accusations are also directed towards people seeking to live somewhere longer-term.

Since the laws around sex work differ wildly by country and region, with additional restrictions that prevent known sex workers from travelling to places like the US even for leisure, it is no wonder that many of us seek to work in countries that are more favourable towards selling sex. Some people come to the UK because it's legal to sell sex here (even if not strictly an accepted form of employment according to the terms of their visa) and the hourly rates for selling sex are higher than in their countries of origin. British sex workers also travel abroad for work as a way to capitalize on being considered unique in a new country, benefiting from differences in legislation which don't criminalize brothels. We might eventually move countries to benefit from these laws continuously. Any involvement by someone who facilitates this work will have it labelled trafficking.

Crossing the border often requires the help of a third party to navigate. This is a fact that goes unexamined by people who don't consider the possibility for themselves. Sex workers are very likely to need excuses to enter into a country because we cannot declare our intent to sell sex, as sexual labour isn't accepted, so we will actively look for people willing to facilitate our travel. This order of events is the opposite of what we are told happens with trafficking. Immigrants not selling sex face this problem all the time too, if their skills and professions aren't considered useful enough to contribute to the economy of the country they want to enter.

Hooker Mentality

Typically the utility of a job is assessed based on how much money the position pays and how many vacancies are in the field, so with an oversaturated market like sex work that has inconsistent pay we wouldn't stand a chance irrespective of the stigma around it. Besides the hookers who seek to frame selling sex as a kind of healing or therapy, most of us recognize that it isn't an indispensable service to anyone besides ourselves. Large numbers of agricultural and textile and construction workers are denied visas, who I think we'd have a hard time arguing have jobs less crucial than ours.

On the other hand, our clients often have the kinds of jobs that governments like. Travelling for leisure is of minimal difficulty for them and they're likely to be able to move countries if they have the desire. These clients are the types who would be called expats rather than immigrants if they moved to live out their retirement years. Their goals of engaging in sex tourism and seeking out people of other nationalities to fetishize and purchase cheaper sex from are seen as more respectable than hookers working to survive. These kinds of clients are also prone to bragging about their ability to target young people when going abroad to pay for sex, advising their friends on how easy it is to get away with abusing sex workers when they can hop on a plane home right afterwards and never be identified. I've overheard these conversations at public bars or in workplace smoking areas. The sex workers they travel to see end up on lists and are denied the ability to move to the same countries these clients came from.

Politicians who want to restrict immigration love to frame men of colour seeking asylum or looking to migrate as being sexually predatory, completely ignoring these white men from countries with globally strong passports who are notorious for engaging in sex tourism. Abusing vulnerable people only seems to be treated as a concern when people the government doesn't like are accused of doing it. The difference lies not only in their racism towards Black, Asian and minority ethnic men, but in who is considered an acceptable target. If the victims are cis white girls who wouldn't otherwise have sold sex, there might be an inquiry. Women of colour selling sex, particularly those who are trans, aren't considered worthy of that same feigned attempt at protection. Wealthy white cis women who aren't at any real risk are prioritized at all costs, with immigrant men as the scapegoats.

This framing of immigrant men as dangerous extends beyond claims they will generally be more likely to sexually assault women into assertions that they will traffic them. From there, the rhetoric moves towards the idea that anyone whose parents or grandparents immigrated poses a threat. MPs in the House of Commons pushed for legislation as a result of this rhetoric which would require the publication of sex offenders ethnicities on a quarterly basis, as if this isn't a blatantly racist way to handle data on crime[xxi]. They openly admitted their reasons for doing so were that they believe immigrants and non-white British people are more likely to groom and traffic people via grooming gangs. Such policies make up part of a larger design to treat immigrants as perpetrators of sex trafficking rather than victims of it. People who choose to move to the UK to sell sex for a better quality of life are ignored entirely.

We can trace the current narrative back to the idea of "white slavery" being popularized in 19th and early 20th century Europe as a way to view prostitution among white women. The purpose of calling prostitution among white women a form of slavery was to deny men sexual access to these women outside of marriage and increase the birth rate of white babies. I can see why some people might think this is a leap, but plenty of hookers make a point to know our history and I happen to be one of them. This is all part of the nationalist projects of various states to pressure white citizens into nuclear family structures. Simultaneously, non-white residents have their attempts at forming family units disrupted.

The House of Lords in England formed a committee to investigate white slavery and ultimately crafted the Criminal Law Amendment Act (CLAA) in 1885. Within this act, they defined an involuntary prostitute and created an offence specific to paying women for sex who were not already known to sell it or be promiscuous. Men were not allowed to pay *"any girl or woman under twenty-one years of age, not being a common prostitute, or of known immoral character, to have unlawful carnal connexion*"[xxii]. Restricting women from earning money via one of the only methods available to them without a man functionally owning them made it even harder to escape marriage and potentially deadly childbirth. Coercive forces acted on them from all sides. Patriarchal society tried to force them into marriage and if it failed to do so they were demoted in status to immoral women and collectively viewed as whores. According to the legislation put in place, they'd be viewed this way for having sex outside of marriage without charging! It took decades for these terms to evolve and be replaced with the generic "trafficking". Through these changes, the whorephobic and racist ideals behind the labels stuck.

While wealthy white women who do not sell sex can benefit from these narratives in the modern day by signalling their fear of being trafficked to gain the attention of white suitors, sex workers of all ethnicities and immigration statuses are incentivized to have solidarity. We have already been demoted to the status of common prostitute. Sex workers of colour, particularly those who are immigrants, are cited as the source of this corruption and may be deported or arrested. White sex workers also experience paternalistic control which limits our ability to earn a living, our politicians and police invoking the difficult experiences and trauma of the immigrant sex workers *that our same governments help create* to justify these restrictions.

Far too many times to count I have heard that Black and brown immigrants do not embody "British values", with sex work often stated to be part of this reasoning. I find it laughable they they act as though we don't have a long history of British born and bred working girls and rent boys propping up this country's working class, regardless of race. These values are not those of the average British person – they're the values our government wants to enforce and is trying to manufacture in its populace. All hookers should be able to see that these British values do not include us, meaning we owe them no respect or allegiance. Our cultural upbringing which rejects us should not impact our willingness to welcome our immigrant siblings in the fight for sex worker rights, or indeed any immigrants regardless of what they do for work.

Furthermore, since our jobs are not considered valuable to society or the economy (because so many of us are too scared to pay our earnings into the bank and therefore pay less tax than desired), we have no reason to side with our governments when they insist we should only allow people in high-paying and sorely needed professions to immigrate. We don't meet the standards being imposed. Even those who believe the poorly-constructed lies about immigrants doing harm to the economy by taking jobs that people born in Britain would otherwise be employed in know that they're not one of the people who is imagined to be losing out. If anything, our empathy for fellow humans aside, this rhetoric should make us want immigrants to get on benefits and have easy access to traditional work because it makes our industry less oversaturated if their income is sourced from somewhere other than punters.

In addition to knowing that we are more similar than we are different, immigrant and native populations of sex workers will see each other in brothels, at support groups, in unions, at strip clubs, and on the sites we use to advertise. As over-saturated as sex work can often be, we aren't actually in serious competition. Clients have their niches and a tendency to stick to them. We are all competing with those of similar demographics far more than anyone else. Upon getting to know each other we form strong bonds and are devastated when our friends are deported. Understanding the discrimination against immigrants on an intellectual level is one thing, but knowing someone's working conditions and their struggle and seeing your government do everything they can to make their life harder is harrowing. We all see the vile racism of clients towards racialized and immigrant sex workers on punter forums, in between searching for posts about our work personas, and then we see politicians echo their sentiments with more polite language as they kick those same migrant workers out of the country.

With many of the friends I have made over the years who came to the UK to work, I can imagine them in different circumstances easily. I can picture scenarios where they did not split up with their partners who had steady jobs, allowing them to stay at home with their children without working. Some could have ended up in a totally different profession if even one of their initial job interviews had lead to them being accepted. Others could have avoided selling sex with a little more support from the government or surrounding community when they arrived claiming asylum and weren't legally permitted to work. All of these versions of the people I've known are ones I would have been a lot less likely to meet, as a home body who spent years in and out of brothels instead of more traditional employment, yet they would have been equally as valuable. Their hopes and dreams would have remained similar. If I empathize with them as sex workers, I can do so as *workers* in general or simply as *people*.

When it comes to the immigrants I've met who sold sex both in their home countries and the ones they've moved to, they have shown me that our struggle by region is not as different as we are taught to expect. One slow night, too wired from coke to sleep, I asked a Columbian colleague working from the same flat as me about how she was adjusting to selling sex in a different environment. She told me that the difference between working on the street compared to indoors in Columbia was larger than the difference moving countries and that stuck with me. It wasn't what I expected her to say. Another sex worker at a SWARM event who had come over from Norway told me how client criminalisation made her work challenging, so she was pleased not to suffer it in the UK, but said her approach to activism had remained much the same because so many of our laws were still restrictive. One of my online hooker friends from India still semi-regularly complains to me that he'd always heard sex work was much less of a struggle in Europe, leaving him immensely disappointed when moving to Germany and struggling just as much as he did before.

Not all sex workers agree and immigrants are no more of a monolith, so these examples don't speak for everyone. What they do is paint a picture of a world less divided than radical feminists would have me believe. Sex workers who delve into activism can use our knowledge of these shared experiences to counter trafficking narratives that insist the attitudes of prostitutes are fundamentally different depending on where we come from. We cannot allow all sex workers in the Global South to be painted as a group with no autonomy who are desperate to have their clients arrested. We know this to be a lie because these sex workers are not voiceless; they're out fighting for decriminalization too, screaming and not being listened to! When these same sex workers immigrate, I find no fiercer advocates for our rights as a collective than them. I listen to these immigrants argue against client criminalization and push back on the insistence that we should use broad definitions of trafficking.

Hooker Mentality

Reading about a sex worker rights protest in Nairobi on International Day to End Violence Against Sex Workers (December 17th), shortly after attending my first protest marking that same day in a different year, I was struck by the similarities between our marches and demonstrations all over the world. I absorbed Chi Adanna Mgbako's words[xxiii].

"At Freedom Corner, red umbrellas—the global symbol of the sex workers' rights movement, signifying the beauty and strength of vibrant inclusivity—are strewn all over the dew-laced grass. Signs that read "Only Rights Can Stop the Wrongs!" lie next to the umbrellas. Slowly, sex workers and their allies gather under Wangari's trees, quietly conversing, waiting to begin. They are wearing "Save us from Saviors" pins and t-shirts that read, "No to stigma and discrimination. Yes to life." They inflate condoms and attach them to their clothes. Bright red condom packets with "love" in gold lettering stick out of their sun visors. I notice people carrying rainbow-striped flags, the international symbol of the LGBT rights movement, as an activist proudly tells me, "The sex worker movement and the queer movement basically coexist in Kenya." I'm comforted by the deep solidarity on display."

Under different trees and surrounded by different architecture, I have seen sex workers protest in England

and in France carrying these same red umbrellas and signs with similar slogans. Members of SWASH (a Japanese group of sex workers aiming to improve the health and safety of their community), SWOP (US sex worker outreach project), Red Canary Song (a grassroots collective of migrant massage workers, sex workers, and allies of Asian diaspora), ESWA (European Sex Workers' Rights Alliance) and many more sex worker led groups are all singing from the same hymn sheet on these issues. We're united across borders with the same mission. It's far easier to realize our goals as a network than alone.

From the commonalities in our activism, we can extrapolate that our outlook on prostitution is mostly shared. While the levels of abuse sex workers suffer is higher in some countries, this is the result of less access to resources or money. Within a single country we see disparities between the high-end escorts and survival sex workers following the same patterns. Greater levels of abuse tend to result in stronger demands for rights because of how urgently they are needed, not backtracking and pleading for our clients to be treated as criminals.

Considering the real reasons for worse conditions in sex work and our awareness of this, closed borders feel more like a punishment than a safety measure. All a restriction on sex workers migrating causes is a denial of the possibility for us to engage in the same practices we already do in a country we choose for slightly better laws and higher pay. With access to these things and the ability to cross borders without aid, we are at less risk of exploitation by traffickers! If governments honestly wanted to make the end of forced sexual labour into a priority, they'd be lessening all restrictions on immigration.

Armed with the truth that anti-immigration laws protect neither potential victims of forced labour who are trafficked nor the sex workers native to a country, hookers can shed any lingering attachment to them that results from a life of nationalist indoctrination. The knowledge that these excuses about protecting prostitutes are made up as a cover for racism spreads to our thoughts on every immigration issue. Building a country where people want to immigrate to improve their lives should be a point of pride, not something to dissuade as we gatekeep our resources and land.

Chapter 8:
Youth Liberation

If I mention child labour, people know what I mean and don't tend to question that it is a form of work. It is exploitative because it involves children whose energy should be spent on learning and developing rather than financially providing for themselves and their families. Sweatshops and mines are the first workplaces which come to mind for many people in North America or Europe who want to think of child labour as an exclusively foreign problem, but there are of course far more varied jobs that children do and each involves a different level of abuse. We also don't have to look abroad to find children working.

There are innumerable children (those below the age of majority) who sell sex to earn enough to survive. These teen sex workers are some of the most vulnerable, not least because their work fundamentally involves grooming and sexual assault. Referring to those under their countries' ages of consent or adulthood as being capable of selling sex does not imply that the clients who take them up on the offer are not rapists. All it does is acknowledge the element of this exchange which is compensated labour.

Rape is sex without consent, in the simplest terms. The reason to oppose sexual assault and rape being referred to exclusively as "sex" is that it leaves out the mention of any force or coercion behind the assault. When we say a person was forced to perform sexual acts, this minimization is not occurring. If you are sensitively discussing young people under the age of consent selling sex, the same applies. The alternative, to insist that a child sells their own rape rather than sex, frames a child who seeks out clients on their own as asking to be sexually assaulted. Refusing to discuss the child's actions at all and only framing the discussion around what the client does means denying victims the language to describe their own experiences, creating a lexicon that exists purely to speak over them. A child can sell sex and an adult commits a rape if they buy it from them. We can use both phrases in the same conversation and neither becomes false purely because it is horrifying to say.

A distinction must also be acknowledged between teens who independently sell sex and those who are controlled or literally sold and passed between traffickers. A child who has their time sold by a third party and keeps none of that money is not a sex worker in any sense of the word, they are sexually enslaved.

Their need to be freed from the control of their abusers is obvious and simplistic. When considering the needs of those under the age of 18 who sell sex as a means to earn money for survival, the issue becomes more complicated and we find ourselves with some shades of grey.

People with extremely traumatic experiences selling sex before they reached adulthood may not want to conceptualize what happened as a kind of work, regardless of how much choice they had in the matter. Children paid to sell drugs or toil in mines also may not view this as a form of work. The differentiating factors as to how young people conceptualize the exploitation they are facing when they perform labour are how those around them see it and whether there is shame associated with the work. Many are rightfully afraid that calling their experiences sex work will be seen as condoning the abuse that happened to them, sanitizing it, because the people they are surrounded by have not reckoned with the horrors that many people experience precisely because what they are doing is work.

Children get into sex work for a plethora of reasons. The biggest driving force is financial need, the same as for those older than them. That financial need tends to be created because children are systemically failed by the adults and structures that are supposed to protect them. In the absence of care systems which adequately support them, the youth population turning to hooking continues to grow.

Hooker Mentality

Impoverished young people are subject to unintentional neglect from parents trying to provide for them on a constant basis. There are countless parents who cannot afford childcare or give their child a comfortable life and must spend long hours working to secure the bare minimum of food and a roof over their heads. Other children have abusive parents who ignore their needs due to a lack of care and withhold money from them. Whichever the case may be, these young people end up being left without supervision for long periods of time and develop a strong desire or need for money. Sometimes these young people are removed from homes like these to be placed into the care of the state, only to end up dealing with the same kinds of emotional and physical neglect alongside a need for money that is just as substantial.

Predators find teens who are in desperate need of money and offer it to them in exchange for sexual services. This is the primary way that they are introduced to the idea, contrary to the popular narrative that our youth flock to the job because of seeing sex work glamourized on social media. The first offer like this will probably make the young person run in a panic or block the predator online, however the insidious nature of this kind of grooming is that it plants the idea. With one offer, the minor becomes aware that if they began selling sex there would be people willing to pay them. They even have a sense of where they might find more adults who are interested in becoming their clients, based on wherever the initial instance of predation occurred.

Every underage sex worker has their catalyst moment. Some become worn down by each attempt at abuse until they decide they need the money enough to accept, while others start to seek clients when a specific monetary goal becomes a focus for them. Perhaps they're kicked out of home and find themselves trading sex for a bed to sleep in, or they need a computer for school that their parents can't afford to buy them. As soon as they begin to sell sex, they're burdened with keeping it a secret.

Knowing that conditions of poverty and neglect are what lead these young people into sex work, the instinct many people have is to insist children must be removed from homes where they face these challenges. It is a quick answer, though not an effective one, because it presumes we have a safer and healthier environment to place them in. In the absence of friends or relatives who can provide a stable life, the traumatic upheaval from their home into foster care where the conditions are equally bad or worse is no solution at all. In an age where we're all connected through the internet, it has also become exceptionally easy for predators to track foster kids they've identified as vulnerable and follow them from placement to placement.

I personally started selling sex when I was made homeless at 17. Since getting to know other sex workers, and because I am so vocal about when I started, I've met many who began selling sex younger than I did and who've shared their stories with me. It's not as common as sex work abolitionists would have you believe for people to start selling sex as children and teens, though it does happen and we need to reckon with it. Among those of us who did, we frequently start out by refusing to examine the reality of our work and denying that we are engaging in prostitution. Once we become adults who continue to sell sex, we eventually reach a point where we have to unpack our childhood experiences and work through what lies underneath our past denial.

Victims of child sexual exploitation who sold sex exclusively whilst underage are most likely not to see their time selling sex as a form of child labour, because nothing compels them to look at their trauma through the lens of an exploited worker. Society's disgust towards prostitutes can be circumvented this way with some people. By refusing to admit to ourselves that we were sex workers of any kind, we may more often be rightfully viewed as victims. It is a survival tactic and a method of coping, because others will not consider underage sex work to be the kind of traumatic experience that it is unless it is only described as rape and no additional context is provided.

According to the law in the UK and many other places, anyone who sells sex before turning 18 is considered a sex trafficking victim. This is the case even when there is no third party involvement. Much like laws which technically label teenagers as perpetrators of creating child pornography for taking nude selfies, these teenagers are being cast in the role of their own traffickers. Fortunately we're not targeted by the law as such. 16 and 17 year olds, who are above the age of consent in the UK for non-transactional sex, are included in this group because there is a higher age requirement for sex which involves a financial exchange. By taking on the label of child sex trafficking victim, those of us who want to dodge some of the stigma associated with sex work are able to.

Once the sexual exploitation begins, child sex workers find it difficult to leave the industry. A lack of access to many of the options that adults have leaves teens especially vulnerable. Minors who have been made homeless or who are expected to fend for themselves are in the worst situation of all, since they can't rely on caregivers and usually can't get another job that will cover their expenses. Children don't have the right to rent a home for themselves and they cannot open a bank account or obtain identification without parental consent. With food and school costs piling up, what money-making avenues are open to a teenager who doesn't want to be placed under the care of social services?

I was very fortunate to have a full-time job at 17 when I was kicked out of home, alongside some savings that my mother failed to intimidate me into returning to her. I worked at a trampoline park frequented mostly by young children. I still ended up selling sex very quickly because the minimum wage for under-18s was only £3.87 an hour at the time for doing exactly the same work as my older colleagues who were paid at least £6.70. The excuse for this minimum wage disparity by age, then and now (though the amounts have increased), was that the lower rate of pay for young people would encourage businesses to hire and train us to get work experience on our CV. This comes with the assumption that teenagers do not have their own bills to pay and will not be demoralized by the abysmal pay. Comparing the average hourly rate for selling sex to the minimum hourly wage shows a dramatic difference for adults, so it shouldn't be hard to imagine how much bigger it is for a kid who can't hope to earn the same amount from a traditional job.

Co-workers of mine who were also teens were jealous of my sex work, which we all spoke about as sugaring and "scamming old men" at the time. I found our boss on the website I was using, listed as a sugar daddy, and showed them all to illicit shock and awe at my sleuthing skills. I spoke openly about how much money older men were paying me to go out with them, downplaying the sexual elements of the transactional relationship without denying them, and a few of these other teens were openly envious of the freedom this additional work granted me in terms of my financial independence. I was a homeless teenager doing work they were disgusted and fascinated by in equal measure, that they would not consider for themselves, but their desire to obtain my level of self-reliance was undeniable.

Misrepresenting this work to my peers was something I did consciously, yet to some extent I did buy into my own claims. I insisted that I was selling my time rather than sex itself. Any time I worried about turning it down, with the knowledge that I wouldn't be paid if I stopped all the sexual interactions with these clients, I went straight back into denial afterwards. Sex was something I told myself I was offering to encourage a little more generosity or the longevity of my arrangements, not something I wanted to admit was essential to them. Being paid on a weekly or monthly basis regardless of how many times I met these clients in person solidified my ability to sell this lie to myself. As long as cash wasn't placed into my hands in the moments before a sex act, my state of denial could remain intact.

I can confidently say that my life would look extremely different if the job I had at 17 paid me just as much as my adult co-workers. I vividly recall sitting on the train to meet with my first client and shaking with terror as if anticipating the sexual assault I would experience later that evening. I told myself that I couldn't afford to turn around because he was offering me twenty times the rate I earned at the trampoline park I was exhausting myself by working at. Had I been paid more, I'd never have signed up to Seeking Arrangement and I doubt I'd ever have sold sex.

The day I came to view myself as a hooker, regardless of my reticence to sell sex and the denial I'd been in before that point, sticks out in my memory because of how suddenly it happened. A former friend of mine was upset with me because our group of friends had chosen to side with her ex-girlfriend rather than her when the two of them broke up (yes, very petty teenage drama) and so she chose to tell her mother all about me selling sex. I was a couple of months away from being 18 years old and had finally been given a flat within a supported housing unit run by the council. Her mother called me unexpectedly and began ranting about how I was a terrible influence who had turned all of her daughter's friends against her. During this tirade, she revealed that she knew I'd been selling sex and intended to report me for it.

Dread took over my body and I remember feeling all my blood drain out of me. My breath escaped me. I had so little control over my life that I was slowly clawing back and the idea of police intervention for selling sex only terrified me. I was horrified by the realization that her hatred of sex workers took precedent over the victim role I had expected to be cast in. At 17, I didn't think I'd be blamed. Despite this, the words that came out of my mouth to bluff confidence that I could handle the police weren't, "I'm underage, I wouldn't be in trouble," or "I'm not selling sex, I'm only selling my time." Instead, I told her "it's not illegal to sell sex," and that was the first time I acknowledged what I was really doing.

Unfortunately, that moment of clarity did nothing to sway the adult more than twice my age who was yelling at me down the phone. Once she was convinced I was not lying about selling sex being legal in the UK, something I had only learned for myself weeks prior, her next tactic was to suggest calling social services on me. To my friend's mother, I was old enough to be considered immoral for being a prostitute and held accountable for that whilst simultaneously being young enough to control like a naughty child acting out. Social services were a weapon available to her because of the span of a mere couple of months, after which I'd be seen as an adult in the eyes of the law.

I falsified confidence and reminded her that because she'd very briefly housed me when I first became homeless, before another friend's mother took me in, that calling social service put her at risk too. I highly doubt the police would have cared to open an investigation or that she would have faced any consequences, but it was true that I'd sold sex while I was living under her roof. Only a threat impacting her personally seemed to get through to her, rather than the plight of the struggling teenager whose heart was beating out of their chest. She gave up on harassing me out of fear of state intervention that she was at no real risk of.

Hooker Mentality

Having experienced all of that, I'm never going to be able to buy into narratives that teens must be controlled and reported when it is discovered that they're doing some form of sex work. At the same time, I vehemently condemn the adult clients seeking out these teenagers to take advantage of. The trauma I experienced during my first year selling sex is something I have never gotten over. How do we marry together these two perspectives in a way that's cohesive? Personally, I do so by reckoning with the knowledge that carceral systems do not protect our youth from sexual predation. They certainly did not protect me, no matter how I begged. We have to empower young people to protect themselves and build communities which keep them safe. Harm reduction may not be harm eradication, but it's a lot better than what our youth have now.

To offer our aid to minors in these positions, we need large structural change rather than personal interventions which may be punished. Anyone who is aware that a sex worker is under the age of majority, regardless of whether that is above the age of consent where they live, is placed in a position where providing support would be considered inappropriate and could lead to serious consequences. Parents have to weigh up the risk of housing an underage sex worker when social services might decide they aren't doing enough to stop their work and deem them unfit to care for their own children too. Any material help which entangles an adult in a young sex worker's life will result in proximity to the police if their work becomes known.

Providing specific advice to teen sex workers leads to further issues: suggesting the use of an escort advertising website where the users charge higher hourly rates, allowing them to work less, could be viewed as encouragement to sell sex rather than harm reduction; discussing personal experiences that are positive within earshot of them garners accusations of glamourizing the job; offering to be a safety buddy so that someone always knows where they are could be seen as aiding or even controlling elements of their prostitution. The measures which reduce the child's exposure to predators gets the people helping them labelled as predators themselves.

Narratives around the pimp lobby and the idea that sex worker activists are groomers seeking to bring new people into the industry leads to a fear of supporting young people who sell sex that is even more extreme than among the general public. Social events for sex workers are exclusive to adults by default, as are support services which may or may not be run by current or former workers ourselves. It doesn't matter whether there's nudity or adult material present or if it's just a free meal shared among people in the industry who are struggling. To access any level of our camaraderie these teens have to continue to lie about their age. Advice they seek from other hookers in those circumstances cannot take into account the rights they lack due to still legally being considered children, so swathes of it are rendered ineffective.

Luckily there are options other than going to other sex workers for help, in the form of charities and therapists. Or rather it would be lucky they exist if under-18s could actually use them. Mandated reporting leaves social workers with their hands tied, unable to offer aid without getting the police or social services involved and making the teenager's life worse. God forbid the young person is combative and finds it infantilizing to be told what to do with their body after already becoming accustomed to selling sex. These teens are not convenient victims who will beg for any way out of selling sex; they're usually so used to fending for themselves that the idea of being denied their autonomy strikes them as worse than whatever they're going through already. Trauma survivors rarely have easily managed emotions and the younger they are the more volatile those emotions can be.

The plight of child sex trafficking victims is not in opposition to the fight for sex workers' rights. Underage sex workers do not begin selling sex because the industry is legitimized too much or widely accepted, neither of which is true, but because children are systematically oppressed and left without better options and at the mercy of adults who are often predators. The more we stop people with the means and expertise to actually help these teens from doing so, the more likely that the people they do find offering help will be abusers in disguise.

What a sick joke it is that policies put into place with the supposed goal of protecting children from sexual abuse and grooming into prostitution only make them more likely to sell sex. Children are removed from loving homes and placed with abusive parents who their primary caregivers have tried to protect them from, all because the parent who initially had custody is a sex worker and the government is convinced that this is a danger to them. Others are put into care to keep them far from the parent who was working to put food on the table like anyone else. Meanwhile, children in these circumstances are far more likely to turn to selling sex themselves. This is so well-known to be the case that pimps actively seek out young people in the foster system or within abusive households to recruit.

Children are underpaid with the excuse of securing experience for their future employment. Employers break labour laws and try to get the children they do manage to employ to do more hours because it saves them money, causing their education to deteriorate in favour of focusing on work. This pushes them out of the traditional workforce and into sex work and drug dealing and theft as better paid alternatives. Liberation for young people is the only solution.

When a young person has the right to work, they should be paid the same for that work as anyone else. Children without viable caregivers who demonstrate the ability to be self-sufficient should be able to legally emancipate themselves without a long and arduous process, rather than be forced into care. Parents who cannot afford to take care of their children should be provided with the funds to do so, rather than having their children taken away and looked after through a process which costs more money than the alternative. School meals should be free and readily available to children without means testing, as should transportation and any tools and technology necessary for learning.

I should not have had to sell sex as a teenager so I would have food in my stomach or a bus ticket to get to school or a laptop for college. Those things should have been provided for me and they should be provided now for every child. I should have been better educated on ways I could keep myself safe and advised not to make myself more of a target by sharing my age with clients. If sex worker advocacy groups were able to do outreach to people in my age group back then, including in colleges and schools, I would have been.

The shock and horror of those who have never sold sex underage doesn't do minors selling sex any good if it leads to more smothering of their rights and autonomy. Children engaging in sex work is a symptom of children's general oppression, not a phenomenon that children and their allies should be restricted even more strongly to prevent.

Chapter 9:
Pathologization

For as long as humans have existed, some of us have been considered mad. This madness has historically been blamed on supernatural forces, the moon, and now on chemical imbalances or abnormal structures within the brain. Modern psychiatry seeks to categorize those of us viewed as mad, as a result of our actions or the thoughts we admit to having, and to medicate us or provide us with therapy so that we become productive members of society. Sometimes these treatments align with our goals and the diagnoses slot right into our self-concept, and other times this focus on making us into ideal members of society according to the state or psychiatrists on power trips is destructive.

From the inception of our modern psychiatric texts such as the ICD (International Classification of Diseases), DSM (Diagnostic and Statistical Manual of Mental Disorders) and the CCMD (Chinese

Classification of Mental Disorders), whorephobia has permeated the ideas within. This can be traced back to some of the first texts on sexual pathology, such as Psychopathia Sexualis written by Richard von Krafft-Ebing.

During the late 19th century, when the idea of paraphilias was becoming more mainstream as an explanation for certain sexual behaviours, we became to see modern psychiatric practices emerge. Sexual interests were measured up against a normative sexuality that had been long-established, with deviance being assumed to be a result of temptation by the devil towards sin or of sickness. Doctors primarily concerned themselves with the paraphilias that men experienced, because women were not seen as complex moral beings and their normative sexuality featured a lack of desire. Women's sexuality was expected to be reciprocal to what was imposed upon them by men, as if the entire gender is only a canvas to be painted upon, and so men and the culture they had formed received the blame for the supposed sickness of prostitution and of female prostitutes.

Lesbianism among sex workers has always been commonplace. Astute researchers in the modern day are likely to theorize that in the present and the past, this prevalence of lesbians selling sex to men is both a method for avoiding marriage and being controlled by a singular man as well as a result of discrimination towards lesbians in the workforce. Naturally, the doctors who birthed modern psychiatry didn't see things that way and instead saw lesbianism as a sickness caused by the sadism of men paying for sex. We can find this stated clearly among the pages of Psychopathia Sexualis:

"According to this experienced author, repugnance for the most disgusting and perverse acts (coitusin axilla, inter mammae, etc.) which men perform on prostitutes is not infrequently responsible for driving these unfortunate creatures to Lesbian love. From his statements it is seen that it is essentially prostitutes of great sensuality who, unsatisfied with intercourse with impotent or perverse men, and impelled by their disgusting practices, come to indulge in it."[xxiv]

Perversions attributed to clients were seen as akin to a communicable disease which women selling sex could absorb, only to end up enacting the same carnal relations with other women as if their actions based on desire were symptoms. These ideas might not be clearly stated in psychiatric texts written over a century later, but the ideas underpinning these beliefs remain. Any behaviour outside of what is considered acceptable will be compared to the conceptual ideal and from there an explanation must be found for it, so hookers end up with psychiatrists fishing for trauma to point to as a source for what they label as sickness.

Hooker Mentality

Actions taken logically by sex workers in pursuit of money are assumed to be a result of impulse or heightened emotional states, because no exceptions are made in the diagnostic criteria for people who have selling sex as a profession. Psychiatrists are unwilling to differentiate between the pursuit of multiple sexual partners as a result of hypersexuality stemming from trauma and sex workers who sleep with multiple people for money. It is as if the action is more important than reason. They follow Freud's lead and allow their biases to govern what they attribute their clients' conduct to.

Nowadays mental illnesses are understood to be caused by chemical imbalances and changes in the brain resulting from environmental factors including trauma. Psychiatrists and other mental health professionals assess whether someone has these issues by looking at lists of symptoms and matching them to what someone says and how they act, without consideration for how circumstances rather than someone's brain itself might result in certain behaviours and thoughts. For sex workers, this leads researchers to suspect high rates of depression[xxv], anxiety, PTSD and BPD[xxvi].

Rejections of such labels are written off as a result of a distrust of doctors which is presupposed to be irrational. We are considered too ill to recognize our own illnesses. This leaves us free to reject their input entirely and to understand our mental health in the way which makes the most sense for us, including self-diagnosis or self-medicating, because the system

178

becomes something to be worked around instead of something to be used. Labels become useful only for finding community rather than seeking medical support, because having a diagnosis on file is a fast track to having our material concerns ignored as the product of over-reactions.

Is it disordered to be anxious while engaging in risky behaviours which we'd be punished for if caught? I met every criterion for the diagnosis of an anxiety disorder when I was bringing new clients into my home every day, being mistreated semi-regularly and spied on by disapproving neighbours. Once I moved and stopped selling sex from my own home under those circumstances, the constant fear dissipated because I was no longer in the situation causing it. Clinicians would also have described me as depressed when I was being harassed by various ex friends and family members over my profession, but again I was only responding to my environment. It is not evidence of a chemical imbalance to be upset when something upsetting is happening. All sorts of marginalized people will be familiar with diagnoses being pushed upon them in this way. There is a failure to consider that sometimes constant fear or upset is totally rational.

When it comes to our sexual behaviours and the reactions we cultivate to cope with abuse from clients or the stigma, that is where we see the puritanical underbelly of psychiatry reveal itself. Dissociation we learn to trigger to make clients easier to deal with is treated as a pathological state. Strong emotional reactions to perceived threats are assumed to be unreasonable rather than learned responses to red flags which keep us safe. Our actions can be entirely calculated and intentional but still end up being treated as a sickness because they're out of line with what is deemed societally acceptable.

In the aftermath of sexual assault, sex workers' mental health is especially scrutinized. We react too little or we react too much. No reaction to sexual assault from a sex worker will be considered correct, because we are automatically not perfect victims. Blaming ourselves is expected, yet it is viewed as hypocrisy because we have chosen a profession where the rate of sexual assault is high, leaving us open to accusations of instability and rapidly changing emotions. When we brush it off because we have become desensitized, this is seen as avoidant behaviour resulting from PTSD or a dissociative symptom of some other disorder. Typically the inception of these ingrained responses is assumed to have taken place in childhood.

Childhood molestation is assumed to be a source of many aberrant sexual behaviours. It is a popular homophobic theory that boys are made gay by being sexually abused by men during their formative years and that girls are made into lesbians also through sexual abuse by men. Boys are said to be recreating the trauma as adults and enacting it on others, meanwhile girls are said to be scared away from men entirely. The differing reactions by gender to sexual abuse by men either goes unexamined or is explained away by claims of innate gender differences in the response to molestation. Since the majority of sex workers are women, it might seem unusual that the reasoning given for engagement in sex work more closely matches the narrative used with boys than with girls. We are believed to be repeating the abuse they decide we suffered at a young age as a form of self-punishment, with similar assumptions made across gendered lines because the usual explanations don't fit.

All mental health professionals feel like they need as proof of this pathway into sex work is evidence that a lot of us were abused as children. With data that shows a high enough percentage, they can suggest that the rest of us didn't want to admit to it and have their hypothesis accepted. This would not prove the theorized mechanism behind child abuse victims becoming sex workers, because all it would demonstrate is correlation and not causation, even if the numbers were to be believed. Sexual abuse of children is most likely to happen at the hands of a family member or close family friend, in turn leading to more family dysfunction and higher odds that the victim will not have family support when they are older. One thing we definitively know drives people into sex work is a lack of money or family support when struggling. It is not different from the way that gay children are often targeted by predators because they have more fraught relationships with their parents

181

on average and are less likely to confide in them about the abuse, or because parents themselves seek to punish their gay children over their sexuality.

How we react to trauma isn't a mystery that needs to be solved or traced back to an original incident from which all the bad things in our life stem. PTSD is one of the few diagnostic options which does not posit some foundational issue behind our normal reactions to our day-to-day lives and it still has a huge flaw for a lot of sex workers in dire circumstances; the first letter in the acronym. For sex workers who are being assaulted and abused on a regular basis, the traumatic situation is ongoing and there is no "post" trauma period. For all we know, all of our issues would disappear completely in the aftermath, though I find this unlikely.

Awareness of the limitations of these diagnoses and explanations for our actions doesn't mean that sex workers don't try to access therapy at all. The methods taught for coping with stressful situations or strong emotions can be extremely valuable to people who end up dealing with them often. To get to the point of learning these coping methods, we first have to find a therapist we can open up to and who won't mistreat us because of our work. That is easier said than done.

The way that therapy is set up is not conducive to therapists providing the best quality of care to sex workers who need therapy related to our work. One reason for that which is all but universal is that therapy costs money. Every therapist I've ever had ultimately demonstrated to me that they were uncomfortable with the reality that I have to sell more sex to afford our appointments, knowing that I don't like seeing clients and regularly suffer abuse from them. If I end up having to see an extra client for every therapy session I have, eventually the expense of the sessions results in an assault or an upsetting interaction. The more I share worries over finances, the more I see my therapist doing the maths and the guilt on their face. Notably, this was not an issue I faced while I was in therapy I paid for with customer service work which destroyed my joints and left me in constant pain. That's the kind of suffering that's far more digestible.

Over every session, the question looms as to when the therapist is going to suggest quitting sex work. I wait for them to insist that issues I raise, which I've dealt with since early childhood, are actually the product of prostitution. Not every therapist fails me in the same ways but almost all of them lack the capability to deal with complex cases involving sex workers with compounding traumas. They try to convince me of things that are not true about my life because it's all they've learned how to treat. Because of this, sex workers end up having to educate our therapists about the daily reality of our work and the laws surrounding it just to get something worthwhile out of our sessions down the road. Proactive mental health professionals who have identified sex workers as a group they want to work with might do better than the rest, yet the lack of education on our needs in their initial training tends to shine through.

These biases among therapists and counsellors and psychiatrists can go as far as impacting our lives outside of sessions too, through the issue of when to break confidentiality. Whorephobia can cause strange interpretations of what counts as an intent to harm ourselves or others, as well as of whether we are endangering our children, all of which mental health professionals are mandated to report when they think the issue is serious. A sex working parent who sees clients in the house whilst their child is at school might end up reported to social services based on concerns that a client could show up when the child is home, leading to them being separated. An admission of being pressured by a pimp might result in a call to the police which places the sex worker in a far more precarious working situation. We end up having to watch our words as if we're tip-toeing around the subject of suicide to avoid being thrown in a psych ward, all over the daily realities of our jobs. Only rare therapists who have sex workers in mind will bother to explain how their confidentiality policies would apply to sex work in practice, so we know where we stand and what to avoid saying. Having to ask means we're looked at with suspicion.

This look behind the curtain into how a therapist's training changes their behaviour with clients makes us aware of their fallibility. The more we have to teach them, the more we wonder why we're paying for sessions in place of speaking to a friend. Between that and their legal obligations to be complicit with carceral systems to some extent, we lose the trust instilled in us by people who see therapy as the ultimate fix for mental health issues. Therapy becomes an alternative to be used when the other sex workers in our community are too exhausted to keep talking us through our breakdowns, not a first choice. Once we use our sessions to learn coping methods, we share those insights with peers who don't want to attend.

It is the sex workers who would be considered mad without the context of the job who are the worst off. The assumptions that sex workers are incapable of acting in our own best interests collide with the restrictions on autonomy already normalized for people with mental illnesses deemed the most serious. More visible symptoms make them into targets for the worst clients, push them into homelessness, and people in these circumstances have the sole alternative of being institutionalized in environments where sexual abuse is still rife.

Who is considered to be mad is always shifting. The world of psychiatry does not require a mechanism for how a treatment helps reduce problematic behaviours or thought patterns, only evidence that it ultimately does so. Sex workers are very familiar with how our behaviours are curbed or controlled and reported upon to show a desired outcome. There need not be physical evidence, like with an STI in the past which would have been used as proof of the effects of sin on the mind and body, only the decision to label our undesirable behaviours as a sickness. Since we can be lumped in with the mentally ill at any time, we have a vested interest in solidarity with the mad.

Chapter 10:
Sexual Labour in Utopia

Leftists keep asking "will sex work exist under communism?" or "would sex work exist in your ideal world?" and the only answers I can muster lie somewhere between "who fucking cares?" and "your question is poorly formed." We are suffering in the here and now.

As an umbrella term, sex work encompasses a large range of sexual services. People will obviously continue to put effort into making porn for as long as it remains physically possible, and that is a type of sex work. Performers will include nudity in their acts as a way to entertain. What these leftists who ask whether sex work should exist in a leftist utopia are really asking me is whether physical sex acts would continue to be sold, perhaps for the benefit of the surrounding community.

To estimate whether people would keep doing something recognizable as sex work in a utopia, we first have to determine what we're imagining an ideal world to look like. How a person pictures their ideal world might be shaped in accordance with their political ideology or they might take personal preferences into account.

In a classless and moneyless society, sex could not be sold but might still be traded. In a society where intersex and trans people were accepted and no longer stigmatized, employment discrimination would not collide with fetishization of such bodies to cause us to be disproportionately likely to sell sex. In a society where there was no longer any shame around sex, people would have less need for discretion and control over their sexual partners to feel strong.

Whatever the utopia, the real answer to whether people would trade sex is that they'll do so if there's an incentive. I know that if there were something I sorely desired that I couldn't easily obtain another way, I'd be content to trade sex for it. I would jump to the idea quickly because it's a method I have experience with. Generations down the line, who's to say whether individuals would be so likely to consider trading sex? All I can guarantee is that personally I would keep doing so post-scarcity and with all my needs met for as long as I wanted things which are finite or bespoke. If I adore a particular artist and want an original piece of their work to adorn my wall, that's something there cannot be an infinite amount of. I can't see a compelling argument not to suck dick or clit for it if that's on offer.

Hooker Mentality

Bartering with sex isn't really what people imagine when they try to conceptualize what sex work would look like after a revolution. They may agree fairly easily that bartering with sex would still exist but see this as distinct from a profession. Outside of capitalism I don't see a reason to object to that differentiation as long as the labour is still respected and recognized for what it is, the same as work completed in a home setting like raising children or cleaning and cooking food. To assess whether prostitution might still exist as a job, we have to go deeper and think about the parameters it would exist within.

For some leftists, their ideal society is one where we have abolished money and provide for others according to our ability for the good of the community and with the understanding that we will get what we need in return. A gift economy might exist, though the general idea would be that everyone is cared for without having to rely on personal friends for material aid. Should everything work smoothly as intended, bartering and trade would be a thing of the past. For sexual labour to fit into this world as a job, it would need to be a service people would freely provide for a personal or social benefit to others.

One idea I see people float for how sex work might evolve in this kind of society is that it would become a caring profession or a form of therapy. This already suggests an evolution and required skillset beyond only selling sex. Clients would likely come from the sex worker's local community, hiring them because of a desire for physical intimacy which is impacting them negatively as it goes unfulfilled. Catering to these desires for sexual acts in a safe and non-judgemental environment is hard enough, but providing therapy about sexual hang-ups and constant reassurance alongside it would need to be taught. Saying the wrong things to someone with serious insecurities or mental health issues relating to their sex life can be damaging. Not to mention there's a lot of ethical stickiness that would come with someone fucking their therapist.

The concept of sex workers as a very hands-on version of a sex therapist comes from anecdotes shared by clients and sex workers alike. Certain high-end escorts feel attacked by those who claim their work has no benefit to society, as if that would make them any different from half of the workers across the world, so they insist that they're helping their clients to lead better lives. Upon examining these anecdotes, one common theme I notice is that the mental health improvements claimed to have taken place seem to stem from clients viewing the interest they receive from sex workers as genuine. Meaningless sex culminating in the sense that their partner doesn't actually care about them tends to have the opposite effect. Unlike typical therapists, this means that someone providing sex in a caring capacity would have to feign active enjoyment and interest rather than maintaining a professional distance. This would be a service that relied on clients deluding themselves about why the sex worker was really there, providing a service to the community, to make sure it remained effective.

No thought seems to be spared in this hypothetical for how the sex workers might feel about having to put on an act during sex for these clients, after which they'd be bound by confidentiality not to talk about it. Since most of us wouldn't be lucky enough to be attracted to every client, discomfort can build. Having sex with someone you aren't attracted to when you aren't in a sexual mood can trigger discomfort regardless of how nice the other person is. Hiding this discomfort takes a toll over time. The reason most sex workers tolerate it now is because we're paid for it.

Another idea, posited by people looking to justify the continued existence of sex work by turning it into an essential service, is that it might be a provision for the disabled. Those who cannot move due to quadriplegia or musculoskeletal disorders end up being used as examples of purported undesirables who no-one would want to have sex with and who would be unable to obtain sexual release on their own through masturbation. My instinct is to think about sexual aids which allow disabled people autonomy, so that they can masturbate on their own with privacy rather than rely on another person, and I can't help but wonder if sex workers bodies are been seen as sex toys in this scenario. Others seem to view sex with another person as akin to a need, making the participation of a sexual partner necessary for the disabled person to be fulfilled.

Irrespective of whether we are talking about someone who is disabled that people don't want to sleep with for ableist reasons or someone who people do not want to sleep with because of their abrasive personality, no-one is owed sex with another person and it isn't a requirement for health and happiness. This kind of sexual labour would not be a vital service, nor can I see why having sex with someone who other people don't want to sleep with would be seen as a job without metrics like pay to judge by. Would the community at large appreciate sex workers for doing this and provide for us as a contributor to the community? How would people know this was a task we were undertaking without violating the privacy and dignity of the people we were serving, who apparently have been labelled as undesirables even in a utopian environment?

Perhaps instead the status of sex worker would be given to anyone who made themselves available for casual sex, as long as they were not particularly discriminating about who they would be willing to have sex with. Without police to shut them down, we might see a resurgence of premises once known as houses of ill repute where people gather for sex or orgies. How, under those conditions, would we determine who is performing the labour? This might be a matter of who seeks pleasure and who is present to provide it whilst satiating their own desires too, however that places the label of sex worker onto someone purely based on their current location. The same two people having sex for the same reasons could swap places in the client/worker relationship over the timing of their arrival at a brothel.

The simple fact of the matter is that the fight for sex worker rights occurs within our current context. Our perceptions of work are capitalist ones which do not map neatly onto completely different structures. Therefore, to answer questions about whether sex work will continue to exist outside of capitalism or in a world without scarcity (artificial or otherwise), we must pinpoint what an individual means when they bring it up. Asking for a definition in reply can lead us to the core of the issue. Once we determine whether their version of sex work would indeed exist, the next conundrum is whether measures should be taken to eradicate it.

What immediately springs to mind when I think about the abolition of prostitution is carceral punishment. Given that this is typically not the proposed solution of leftists who want to build a better world through revolution or constant reform, we have to assume other methods of suppression would be used. I wonder how proponents of abolition picture putting an end to trading sex without damaging their ideal world as much as they think they're improving it, no matter how fundamentally incompatible they think the sale of sex is with their utopia.

Hooker Mentality

Exiling clients would be akin to the Nordic Model of client criminalisation, with presumably similar outcomes. Treating trades involving sex as rape and rehabilitating the clients would undermine the bodily autonomy of sex workers, spreading like a cancer to other matters like surrogacy and abortion which suffer from similar complaints of doing harm regardless of the wishes of the person experiencing them. Segregating sex workers from the general population for our own protection is also a possibility, but we might keep selling sex by screwing each other and making our own little ecosystem.

The best case scenario I can imagine for attempted abolition is one in which the goal is prevention through education, although this presupposes that there are unique inherent harms to sex work which justify its eradication. We could educate people that men are not entitled to women's bodies or sex, that extorting anyone using something they want or need to extract sex is wrong, and even if everyone agreed we would still see people trading (notably less but still some) sex in situations without these issues.

Part of what makes a world utopian in my eyes is an end to all forms of bigotry. This would change a lot about how sex work functions compared to the way it previously has throughout human history. When I overhear discussions about sexual labour in a utopia, it is with some of these forms of bigotry baked into assumptions about how it would work, like those debating it cannot fathom a post-misogyny and post-racism world. There are mentions of catering to lonely men with no self-awareness as to how the archetype of the man in need of paid intimacy is shaped by misogyny. People discuss sex tourism with the assumption borders would always be closed and that racism and racial fetishization could not be overcome.

Men buy sex so much more than women because they are wealthier and experience less stigma over their sexual desires. In the context of a world with total gender equality, this would no longer be the case. Clients of all genders would be equally capable of agreeing to pay or trade for sex, with sex workers being spread across all demographics. Without restrictions on human movement and discrimination based on race, we also wouldn't see worse outcomes for sex workers of colour or immigrants. Having surpassed all of these challenges, which are not easily tackled but must have been resolved for us to dare call something a utopia, I can see no reason the populace would be convinced that prostitution must be prevented. It would be a simple matter of bodily autonomy.

Regrettably, utopia is a long way off. All these hypotheticals do is tie us up in knots working out what is and is not the effect of culture and societal conditioning. The question of whether sex work might exist in a better world is a distraction from the world we live in where people are currently suffering, typically posed by those who are uncomfortable reckoning with that reality. They want to picture paying for sexual services without their current guilt. Some seem to believe that giving us the ability to discuss how we might work in a world without stigma will lead to us conceptualizing sex work as necessary, thereby assuaging any lingering concerns about whether they're contributing to a problem with their purchases or viewing of entertainment.

Before I can get to imagining a world where no-one desires to sell sex and the work dies out, I need to be shown a world where no-one *needs* to sell it. My wildest dreams are those where our stomachs are always full and we have roofs over our heads without ever having to think about who we'll fuck for the money. I live in desperate hope for a future where people aren't criminalized and deported and killed and beaten because we're seen as disposable. Pose the question, "would sex work exist in a utopia?" to me and I'll ask myself why that's what you're spending your time asking instead of "how can I help sex workers now?"

About the Author

Jack Parker (he/they) is a sex worker and writer originally from Essex who has been selling sex in the UK since 2016. Over the years he has done so in brothels, from his own home, and by visiting clients in hotels and residences. What he has learned through these experiences informs his writing and activism alike.

When he is not engaging in sex work or imploring members of the public to listen to his community's demands for rights, Jack spends his time engrossed in fanfiction and obsessing over video game characters.

Find him under the username **mxjackparker** across social media.

If you are interested in reading more of Jack's work, you can read many articles on his website at **jackviolet.com.**

You also have the option of checking out **Working Guys: A Transmasculine Sex Worker Anthology** which Jack edited and wrote segments of. Working Guys is a collection of essays, personal narratives and interviews about the lives of transmasculine sex workers, in their own words. It includes 20 contributors discussing their lives, include the joyful, traumatic, and the moments in between. From selling sex under a female persona to taking advantage of the rise in popularity of trans men in porn, the pieces within provide a snapshot of moments in various transmasculine sex workers' lives.

If you have curiosity about the history of sex work, Jack has also translated **Contemporary Prostitution: Study of a Social Question** (1884) by Leo Taxil which covers the sale of sex in 19th century Europe and particularly in France.

i   Economic and Philosophic Manuscripts of 1844, Private Property and Communism by Karl Marx

ii   The Price of Pleasure – Noam Chomsky on Pornography

iii   Women should not be for sale by Julie Bindel, June 2022 – https://thecritic.co.uk/issues/june-2022/women-should-not-be-for-sale/

iv   Andrea Dworkin, Prostitution and Male Supremacy, 1 MICH. J. GENDER & L. 1 (1993). https://repository.law.umich.edu/mjgl/vol1/iss1/1

v   La Prostitution Contemporaine: étude d'une question sociale by Léo Taxil – Translation: Contemporary Prostitution: Study of a social question, pg. 149 – 196.

vi   Crown Prosecution Service, Rape and Sexual Offences – Chapter 6: Consent – Deception as to Sex – https://www.cps.gov.uk/legal-guidance/rape-and-sexual-offences-chapter-6-consent

vii   Secrets and lies: untangling the UK 'spy cops' scandal, The Guardian UK, by Paul Lewis and Rob Evans, 28th October 2020. https://www.theguardian.com/uk-news/2020/oct/28/secrets-and-lies-untangling-the-uk-spy-cops-scandal

viii   https://tryst.link/blog/detained-and-deported-my-experience-at-the-us-border/ - Detained and Deported: My Experience at the US Border by Eddy

ix   Sex-worker charities at loggerheads over work with police, The National, 4th November 2016, https://www.thenational.scot/news/14896756.Sex_worker_charities_at_loggerheads_over_work_with_police/

x   An Independent Review of the Managed Approach to onstreet sex working in Leeds 2014-2020, University of Huddersfield, June 2020, by Jason Roach, Kate Wood, Ashley Cartwright, Barry Percy-Smith, Michelle Rogerson, Rachel Armitage. https://democracy.leeds.gov.uk/documents/s208220/Managed%20Approach%20Independent%20Review%20Report%20Appendix%2020080720.pdf

xi   Bristol's street sex workers helping protect some of the city's most at-risk children, BristolLive, Bristol Post, 7th May 2025, Kirstie McCrum. https://www.bristolpost.co.uk/news/bristol-news/bristols-street-sex-workers-helping-10158442

xii   Farley, M., Cotton, A., Lynne, J., Zumbeck, S., Spiwak, F., Reyes, M. E., … Sezgin, U. (2004). Prostitution and Trafficking in Nine Countries: An Update on Violence and Posttraumatic Stress Disorder. Journal of Trauma Practice, 2(3–

4), 33–74. https://doi.org/10.1300/J189v02n03_03

xiii Farley, Melissa; Banks, Martha E.; Ackerman, Rosalie J.; and Golding, Jacqueline M. (2018) "Screening for Traumatic Brain Injury in Prostituted Women," Dignity: A Journal of Analysis of Exploitation and Violence: Vol. 3: Iss. 2, Article 5. https://doi.org/10.23860/dignity.2018.03.02.05

xiv Brooks-Gordon, Belinda and Mai, N. and Perry, G. and Sanders, T. (2015) Production, income, and expenditure in commercial sexual activity as a measure of GDP in the UK national accounts. Project Report. Office for National Statistics, London, UK. https://eprints.bbk.ac.uk/id/eprint/17962/

xv M. Hester, N. Mulvihill, A. Matolcsi, A. L. Sanchez, S. Walker, University of Bristol (October 2019) – The nature and prevalence of prostitution and sex work in England and Wales today – https://www.gov.uk/government/publications/nature-of-prostitution-and-sex-work-in-england-and-wales

xvi https://nationaluglymugs.org, National Ugly Mugs, Memorial Map and Memorial Card.

xvii RÉPONSES A L'EVALUATION DE LA LOI DE 2016, 22 June 2020, Medecins du Monde. https://www.medecinsdumonde.org/publication/travail-du-sexe-rapport-devaluation-de-la-loi-de-2016/

xviii Aileen: Life And Death Of A Serial Killer.

xix What Prison Taught Me About Love and Sex, Vice, by Sarah Jane Baker, February 4th 2020. https://www.vice.com/en/article/sex-in-prisons-what-prison-taught-me-about-love/

xx Kim S, Johnson TP, Goswami S, Puisis M. Risk factors for homelessness and sex trade among incarcerated women: A Structural equation model. J Int Womens Stud. 2011 https://pmc.ncbi.nlm.nih.gov/articles/PMC3233202/

xxi Crime and Policing Bill (Amendment Paper), Committee Stage: Tuesday 8 April 2025. https://publications.parliament.uk/pa/bills/cbill/59-01/0187/amend/crime_policing_day_pbc_0408.pdf

xxii Criminal Law Amendment Act 1885, UK Public General Acts, Chapter 69. https://www.legislation.gov.uk/ukpga/Vict/48-49/69/enacted

xxiii To Live Freely in This World: Sex Worker Activism in Africa by Chi Adanna Mgbako, Introduction, page 3.

xxiv Psychopathia Sexualis, Richard von Krafft-Ebing, 1886, page 429.

xxv Martín-Romo, L., Sanmartín, F. J., & Velasco, J. Invisible and stigmatized: A systematic review of mental health and risk factors among sex workers. Acta psychiatrica Scandinavica, 2023. https://pubmed.ncbi.nlm.nih.gov/37105542/

xxviIvanich J, Welch-Lazoritz M, Dombrowski K. The Relationship between Survival Sex and Borderline Personality Disorder Symptoms in a High Risk Female Population. Int J Environ Res Public Health. 2017. https://pmc.ncbi.nlm.nih.gov/articles/PMC5615568/